Ropin' the Flavors of Texas

The Junior League is an organization of women committed to promoting voluntarism, developing the potential of women, and improving communities through the effective action and leadership of trained volunteers. Its purpose is exclusively educational and charitable.

Money raised by the sale of *Ropin' the Flavors of Texas* furthers the purpose and projects of the Junior League of Victoria, Texas, Inc.

For additional copies, use the order forms at the back of this book or send a check for $22.95 plus $4.00 shipping and handling (Texas residents add $1.89 sales tax) to:

Ropin' the Flavors of Texas
The Junior League of Victoria, Texas, Inc.
202 North Main Street
Victoria, Texas 77901
361-573-4508
1-877-752-7222

Original Illustrations by Mary Wenske

Library of Congress catalog card number 00-131141

ISBN 0-9608608-1-9

First Edition

First Printing   7,500 copies   October 2000

Printed in the USA by
WIMMER
The Wimmer Companies
Memphis
· 1-800-548-2537

introduction

The Coastal Bend, the Crossroads, the Crescent Valley, the Texas Mid-Coast — these are all designations which refer to the city of Victoria and its surrounding area. Victoria acquires its nicknames from its unique location on the southeast border of the state. It not only lies in close proximity to the Gulf of Mexico, it is virtually centered inside the imaginary triangle formed by the cities of Houston, San Antonio, and Corpus Christi. History is in abundance in this locality of over 60,000 residents, 100,000 countywide. The region that surrounds Victoria was the theatre for much of Texas' struggle for independence from Mexico. Mexican culture and tradition are still of great influence. However, other cultures have settled here, and Victoria is a mixture of many heritages.

Since the time of its earliest settlers, Victoria has continuously developed and matured. As the city has grown over the years, so has its need for effective community service organizations and leaders. Out of this necessity, the Junior Service League of Victoria was formed in 1937. The focus of this new association of young women was child welfare and providing volunteer service for the betterment of the community's children. During its early years, the League subsidized and furnished volunteer assistance for the Victoria County Child Welfare Program. During World War II, efforts of the League concentrated on benefiting the war effort.

After the war, the League was once again able to concentrate on the needs of the community's children. In the years that followed, it was instrumental in establishing, funding, and providing volunteer service for numerous projects which served the medical, educational, and emotional needs of children. In more recent years, the League has expanded their focus areas to include educationally at-risk youth, the environment, and health and wellness. The League's latest undertaking is the collaboration and construction of an all-women built home with the Victoria Chapter of Habitat for Humanity. In addition, numberless community organizations benefit from both financial contributions and volunteer assistance provided by the League.

Because of its affiliation with the Association of Junior Leagues International in 1983, the organization became the Junior League of Victoria, Texas, Inc. and is currently headquartered in the historic O'Connor-Proctor Building in downtown Victoria. In order to provide funding for its numerous undertakings, the League has hosted a variety of creative fundraising events over the years. Most notable is the Charity Ball which has been an annual event since 1960. Most recently, the membership approved an additional endeavor, the development and publication of a new cookbook. The outcome of this decision is ROPIN' THE FLAVORS OF TEXAS, *Culinary Creations from the Coastal Bend*. This is not the first time, however, that the League has tackled this venture. In 1982, ENTERTAINING IN TEXAS was issued, and a sample of some favorite recipes is included in this new publication. Monies raised by these, as well as all fund-raising efforts, are put back into the community through League sponsored projects and the Community Assistance Fund.

cookbook committee

Jackie Marlow	Beth Antimarino
Melanie Buchhorn	Diane Alexander
Jill Lau	Brenda Hermes
Mary Schuenemann	Jennifer Camet
Kelly Sowell	Jill Schlein

sustaining advisors

Gormeen Kamin   Tenna Thompson

about the artist

Mary Wenske grew up in Southern California, where she developed a love for the Spanish Missions on the California Coast. She began her art studies at Cal-State Fullerton College. Being a 6th generation Texan, Mary's family heritage brought her home to South Texas, there she enrolled in Victoria College, then Southwest Texas State University to pursue her career in art. The mother of seven children, Mary uses her creative skills in various projects. She volunteers her talent to a variety of organizations, school and church functions. In her spare time she has traveled from South Texas to San Francisco, painting works of art for friends and family in their homes. *Ropin' the Flavors of Texas* is Mary's first "Taste" of illustrating a cookbook. Her love of bright colors and western flair are what make *Ropin' the Flavors of Texas* so inviting. Mary's professor in college once said that he was going to read about her one day-we hope he cooks!

The cookbook committee would like to thank Mary for all of her creative ideas and hard work that she put into making *Ropin' the Flavors of Texas,* a cookbook for all to enjoy.

Contents

As the committee struggled to develop a title for this cookbook, members often stumbled over the subtitle, *Culinary Creations from the Coastal Bend,* inadvertently substituting the word *blend* for *bend.* The word *blend,* however, adequately describes this region of Texas. Victoria, as well as the entire state, is a blend of heritages – and the cuisine a blend of tastes and flavors. *ROPIN' THE FLAVORS OF TEXAS* captures this unique mix, and shares recipes which exemplify the variety found in cooking across Texas' kitchens today. Over 800 recipes were submitted from League members, their families, and friends. Of the recipes received, over 300 were selected. Each was thoroughly tested and chosen not only because of great flavor, but also because of its ease of preparation and attractiveness in presentation. Some dishes are more elegant for entertaining; others make great family fare. All are delicious and well worth the cooking experience. It is the committee's sincere wish that you will explore the unique blend of flavors and cooking adventures that are offered throughout this cookbook.

ENJOY!

Designates a recipe reprinted from the Junior League of Victoria's 1982 publication, *ENTERTAINING IN TEXAS.*

Appetizers and Beverages

garden salsa

yields approximately 2 quarts

10-12 tomatoes, quartered
24   serrano peppers, halved and seeded
12   jalapeño peppers, halved and seeded
4-6   cloves garlic, peeled

1   cup loosely packed fresh cilantro leaves
1   tablespoon salt
2   teaspoons ground cumin
¾   teaspoon black pepper
2   (15-ounce) cans tomato sauce

Position knife blade in food processor; add tomatoes and process until coarsely chopped. Transfer tomatoes to a large bowl.

Add peppers, garlic, cilantro, salt, cumin and black pepper in food processor. Process until coarsely chopped, adding ¼ cup water, if necessary.

Stir pepper mixture into tomatoes; add tomato sauce, stirring until well blended. Cover and refrigerate several hours to allow flavors to blend.

If not using immediately, pour salsa in heavy-duty plastic freezer bags and freeze. To serve, defrost and remove excess liquid to maintain desired consistency. Salsa may be processed in canning jars according to manufacturer's recommendations.

★ *poquito mas* ★

Serrano peppers-The serrano is a small, light green chili pepper that is very hot. As it matures, it turns from bright green to scarlet red, then yellow. Look for chiles that are 1½ to 3 inches long and ½-inch wide with smooth skins and white seeds.

southwestern salsa

yields approximately 1 quart

2   (10-ounce) cans diced tomatoes with green chiles
2   (14.5-ounce) cans diced tomatoes
6   Roma tomatoes, diced
1   large onion, diced

2   bunches green onions, chopped
2   bunches fresh cilantro, chopped
2   teaspoons ground cumin
    salt
    pepper

Combine tomatoes, onions, cilantro and cumin in a large bowl. Season to taste with salt and pepper. Cover and refrigerate until ready to serve.

Serve with tortilla chips or Tex-Mex food.

corn salsa

yields approximately 1 quart

2   (11-ounce) cans white shoepeg corn
2   cucumbers, chopped
2   carrots, peeled and chopped
2   avocados, peeled, seeded and chopped
2   Roma tomatoes, chopped

2   serrano peppers, seeded and chopped
½   bunch fresh cilantro, chopped
1-2 lemons, halved
    garlic salt

Combine corn, cucumber, carrot, avocado, tomato, pepper and cilantro in a large bowl. Squeeze lemon juice over mixture and stir. Season to taste with garlic salt, mixing well.

Cover and refrigerate 8 hours or overnight for best flavor. Stir in additional lemon juice and garlic salt, if desired. Serve with tortilla chips.

spicy corn dip

yields approximately 1 quart

2 (11-ounce) cans Mexican style corn, drained
2 (4-ounce) cans chopped green chiles
2 cups (8 ounces) shredded cheddar cheese
1 cup sour cream
1 cup mayonnaise
2 slices fresh jalapeño, seeded and chopped
1 teaspoon cayenne pepper
1 teaspoon garlic powder

Combine corn, chiles, cheese, sour cream, mayonnaise, jalapeño, cayenne pepper and garlic powder in a large bowl.

Cover and refrigerate 8 hours or overnight. Serve with corn or tortilla chips.

texas caviar

yields 8 to 10 servings

½ cup olive oil
¼ cup red wine vinegar
⅛ teaspoon hot sauce, or to taste
2 (15-ounce) cans black beans, rinsed and drained
2 (11-ounce) cans Mexican style corn, drained
2 medium tomatoes, chopped
1 red bell pepper, chopped
1 cup chopped fresh cilantro
½ cup chopped red onion
4-6 teaspoons minced garlic
2 large avocados, peeled, seeded and chopped

Combine olive oil, vinegar and hot sauce; set aside.

Combine black beans, corn, tomato, pepper, cilantro, onion and garlic in a large bowl. Add dressing, tossing to coat.

Cover and refrigerate for 2 hours. Toss in avocado just before serving. Serve with tortilla chips.

dill dip

yields 2 cups

1 cup mayonnaise	1 teaspoon dried dill weed
1 cup sour cream	1 teaspoon dried parsley
1 tablespoon shredded green onions	½ teaspoon Ac'cent
1 teaspoon Beau Monde seasoning	½ teaspoon Worcestershire sauce
1 teaspoon seasoned salt	2 drops hot sauce, or to taste

Combine mayonnaise, sour cream, green onion, seasoning, seasoned salt, dill, parsley, Ac'cent, Worcestershire and hot sauce in a medium bowl.

Cover and refrigerate until ready to serve. Serve with fresh vegetables or bagel chips.

spinach-vegetable dip

yields 8 servings

1 (10-ounce) package frozen chopped spinach, thawed	1 (8-ounce) can water chestnuts, drained and chopped
1 cup sour cream	½ cup shredded carrots
1 (1-ounce) envelope buttermilk dressing mix	1 tablespoon mayonnaise
	1 tablespoon minced onion

Drain spinach, pressing between layers of paper towels; set aside.

Combine sour cream and buttermilk dressing mix, stirring until well blended. Stir in water chestnuts, carrot, mayonnaise and onion. Fold in spinach.

Cover and refrigerate for 24 hours for best flavor. Serve with crackers or tortilla chips.

layered greek dip

yields 8 to 10 servings

1	(8-ounce) package cream cheese, softened	1	tablespoon chopped fresh oregano
1½	cups sour cream, divided	2	tablespoons capers, drained
1⅓	cups canned artichoke hearts, chopped and divided	16	green Greek olives, pitted and quartered
8	pepperoncini peppers, seeded and chopped	1	large tomato, chopped
4	hard-cooked eggs, chopped	3	cloves garlic, chopped
16	black Greek olives, pitted and quartered	1	small cucumber, finely chopped
		4	ounces feta cheese, crumbled
3	tablespoons fresh lemon juice	1	red bell pepper, chopped
		2	tablespoons chopped fresh parsley

Combine cream cheese, ½ cup sour cream and half of the chopped artichoke. Spread evenly in a 1½-quart serving dish.

Combine pepperoncini peppers, eggs and black olives; spread on cream cheese layer.

Combine remaining 1 cup sour cream, lemon juice and oregano and spread over pepper layer. Sprinkle evenly with capers.

Layer green olives, tomato, garlic, cucumber, remaining artichoke hearts, feta cheese, bell pepper and parsley over capers.

Cover with plastic wrap and refrigerate 8 hours or overnight. Serve with pita chips.

layered crab spread

yields 6 to 8 servings

1	(8-ounce) package cream cheese, softened
½	cup sour cream
¼	cup mayonnaise
2	teaspoons Worcestershire sauce
2	teaspoons dry onion flakes
¾	cup chili sauce

2	(4¾-ounce) cans crabmeat, drained and flaked
2	cups (8 ounces) shredded mozzarella cheese
	paprika
	fresh parsley

Combine cream cheese, sour cream, mayonnaise, Worcestershire and onion flakes in a bowl. Spread mixture over a 12-inch dish. Spread chili sauce over cream cheese mixture.

Layer crab and cheese over chili sauce; sprinkle with paprika. Garnish with parsley.

Cover and refrigerate at least 2 hours before serving. Serve with crackers.

layered crab-taco dip

yields 8 to 10 servings

2	(6-ounce) cans lump crabmeat, drained or 1 pound fresh crabmeat, picked
1	medium tomato, diced
2	green onions, minced
½	cup diced red onion
½	cup diced cucumber
2	tablespoons chopped fresh parsley
¼	cup lime juice

¼	cup lemon juice
¼	cup orange juice
	salt
	pepper
2	(8-ounce) packages cream cheese, softened
¼	cup mayonnaise
1	avocado, peeled, seeded and diced

Combine crab, tomato, green onion, red onion, cucumber and parsley in a large glass bowl. Stir in lime, lemon and orange juice. Season to taste with salt and pepper. Cover and refrigerate 8 hours or overnight.

Combine cream cheese and mayonnaise. Spread over a large, round platter to resemble a pizza. Cover cream cheese mixture with diced avocado.

Drain crab mixture, discarding liquid. Spread over avocado. Serve with chips.

shrimp dip

yields 2 cups

1	(8-ounce) package cream cheese, softened	4	ounces cooked and peeled shrimp, chopped
1	cup mayonnaise		salt
1	tablespoon finely grated onion		pepper
1	tablespoon Worcestershire sauce		

Combine cream cheese, mayonnaise, onion, Worcestershire and shrimp in a bowl. Season to taste with salt and pepper.

Cover and refrigerate several hours before serving to allow flavors to blend. Serve with crackers or fresh vegetables.

Crabmeat may be substituted for shrimp.

ceviche

yields 4 cups

1½ pounds white fish (such as flounder) or shrimp	1 (5-ounce) jar pitted green olives, drained and finely chopped
10-12 limes	½ bunch fresh cilantro, chopped
3 large tomatoes, chopped	1 teaspoon chopped fresh oregano
1 small onion, finely chopped	1 teaspoon salt

Cut fish into ¼-inch cubes and place in a large, glass bowl.

Cut limes in half and squeeze juice over fish, tossing to coat. Cover and let stand 6 hours at room temperature or overnight in the refrigerator.

Drain and rinse with cold water. Combine fish, tomato, onion, olives, cilantro, oregano and salt. Cover and refrigerate at least 1 hour to allow flavors to blend.

Serve in salad bowls on top of a bed of fresh lettuce or as a dip with corn tortilla chips.

french bread with goat cheese and sun-dried tomato spread

yields 8 servings

1	(11-ounce) package soft, fresh goat cheese	¼	cup sour cream
⅔	cup chopped pecans		black pepper
½	cup drained and chopped, oil-packed sun-dried tomatoes		minced fresh basil
			chopped pecans
4	teaspoons minced fresh basil or 1 teaspoon dried	2	baguettes French bread, sliced

Combine goat cheese, ⅔ cup pecans, sun-dried tomato and 4 teaspoons basil in a medium bowl.

Stir in sour cream to spreadable consistency. Season to taste with pepper. Spoon into a mound in a serving bowl. Cover and refrigerate. Let stand to room temperature before serving. Sprinkle with additional minced basil and chopped pecans. Serve with bread slices.

Recipe may be made two days prior to serving.

goat cheese with sun-dried tomatoes, garlic and rosemary

yields 6 to 8 servings

6   **sun-dried tomato halves (not packed in oil)**

3   **cloves garlic, finely chopped**

1   **tablespoon chopped fresh or dried rosemary**

3   **tablespoons olive oil**

1   **(10-ounce) package goat cheese fresh rosemary sprigs**

Cover tomato halves with boiling water in a small bowl; let stand 5 minutes. Drain and chop tomatoes.

Combine tomato, garlic, rosemary and oil in a small bowl. Cover and refrigerate up to 4 hours.

Place goat cheese on a serving plate and let stand until room temperature. Pour tomato mixture over goat cheese. Garnish with fresh rosemary. Serve with crackers or toasted baguette slices brushed with olive oil.

olive-nut spread

yields 2 cups

1   (8-ounce) package regular or low-fat cream cheese, softened
½   cup mayonnaise
2   tablespoons liquid from jar of green olives

dash black pepper
1   cup chopped green olives
½   cup chopped pecans

Combine cream cheese and mayonnaise in a medium bowl. Stir in liquid and pepper. Fold in olives and pecans.

Cover and refrigerate until ready to serve. Serve with assorted crackers.

pinecone cheese ball

yields 16 servings

1   (8-ounce) container garden vegetable cream cheese
1   (8-ounce) container roasted garlic cream cheese

1   cup (4 ounces) shredded sharp cheddar cheese
3   green onions, chopped
2   cups pecan halves, toasted
    fresh rosemary sprigs

Combine cheeses and green onion; shape into an oval shape on a serving platter. Cover and chill 2 hours.

Arrange pecan halves over cheese in overlapping rows beginning at the bottom to resemble a pinecone. Garnish with rosemary. Serve with crackers.

texas cheese ring

yields 16 to 24 servings

2 (10-ounce) packages sharp cheddar cheese, cut into pieces
½ onion, coarsely chopped
1 cup pecans
⅔ cup mayonnaise

¼ teaspoon garlic salt
¼ teaspoon black pepper
cayenne pepper
roasted raspberry-chipotle pepper sauce or raspberry or strawberry preserves

Position knife blade in food processor; add cheese and onion. Process until blended. Transfer cheese mixture to a large bowl; set aside.

Place pecans in food processor; process until coarsely chopped. Add mayonnaise, garlic salt, black pepper and cayenne pepper; process until finely chopped.

Stir mayonnaise mixture into cheese mixture, mixing until well blended. Shape into a ring on a serving platter. Pour pepper sauce into center of ring. Serve with crackers.

favorite cheese ball

yields 12 servings

2 (3-ounce) packages cream cheese, softened
4-6 green onions, chopped

1 (5-ounce) jar dried beef, chopped
1 teaspoon cayenne pepper
paprika

Combine cream cheese, onion, beef and cayenne pepper in a small bowl. Shape into a ball and sprinkle evenly with paprika. Serve with buttery crackers.

jalapeño cheese dip

yields 8 to 10 servings

6	cups (24 ounces) shredded colby-jack cheese	¼	cup diced white onion
1	(16-ounce) jar mayonnaise	¼	cup diced green onions
1	(4.5-ounce) can chopped ripe olives	2-4	tablespoons diced fresh jalapeños, or to taste
1	(4-ounce) can diced green chiles	2	cloves garlic, minced
1	(2-ounce) jar diced pimientos, drained		

Combine cheese, mayonnaise, olives, chiles, pimientos, onion, jalapeño and garlic in a large bowl.

Cover and refrigerate until ready to serve. Serve with crackers, chips or bagel crisps.

pimiento cheese spread

yields 6 to 8 servings

2½	cups (10 ounces) shredded cheddar cheese	4	ounces diced pimientos, drained
1	cup (4 ounces) shredded mozzarella cheese	4	ounces ripe olives, chopped
½	cup picante sauce	2	large pickles, chopped
			salad dressing or mayonnaise

Combine cheese, picante sauce, pimientos, olives and pickles in a large bowl. Add salad dressing to spreadable consistency.

fiesta cheesecake

yields 16 to 24 servings

1½	cups finely crushed tortilla chips	¼	teaspoon ground red pepper
¼	cup butter, melted	1	(8-ounce) carton sour cream
2	(8-ounce) packages cream cheese, softened	1	cup chopped red or green bell pepper
½	(8-ounce) package cream cheese, softened	½	cup chopped green onions
2	large eggs	1	medium tomato, chopped
2	cups (8 ounces) shredded Monterey Jack cheese with peppers	2	tablespoons finely chopped ripe olives
1	(4-ounce) can chopped green chiles, drained	1	bunch fresh cilantro

Preheat oven to 325°. Combine crushed chips and butter. Press into the bottom of a lightly greased 9-inch springform pan. Bake for 15 minutes; cool.

Beat cream cheese at medium speed with an electric mixer for 3 minutes or until fluffy. Add eggs, one at a time, beating well after each addition. Stir in cheese, chiles and ground red pepper. Pour into prepared pan.

Bake for 30 minutes; cool on a wire rack for 10 minutes. Gently run a knife around the edge of the pan and release the sides. Let cool completely.

Spread sour cream over top; refrigerate until well chilled. Arrange bell pepper, green onion and olives over top of cheesecake. Arrange cilantro sprigs around sides. Serve with tortilla chips.

basil-tomato bruschetta

yields 12 servings

½	cup olive oil	5	medium tomatoes, coarsely chopped
⅓	cup red wine vinegar	⅓	cup pitted ripe olives, sliced
2	tablespoons finely chopped fresh basil	½	cup (4 ounces) feta cheese, crumbled
1	clove garlic, minced	1	loaf Italian or French bread, sliced
⅛	teaspoon coarse ground black pepper		

Combine oil, vinegar, basil, garlic and pepper in a jar. Cover tightly and shake vigorously; set aside.

Combine tomato and olives in a large bowl. Add dressing, tossing to coat. Cover and refrigerate at least 4 hours.

Place a generous amount of the tomato mixture on each slice of bread. Sprinkle evenly with feta cheese.

Broil lightly until toasted. Serve immediately.

cucumber sandwiches

yields 30 finger sandwiches

1	(8-ounce) package cream cheese, softened	½	teaspoon garlic powder
1	cucumber, peeled, seeded and grated	2	tablespoons salad dressing or mayonnaise
2	tablespoons grated onion	1	slice cooked bacon, finely chopped
		12	slices bread

Combine cream cheese, cucumber, onion, garlic powder, salad dressing and chopped bacon in a bowl. Cover and refrigerate until well chilled. Spread mixture on 6 slices bread; top with remaining 6 slices. Trim crusts from sandwiches and cut each into 5 pieces.

marinated shrimp with capers and dill

yields 8 appetizer servings

½	cup plus 2 tablespoons olive oil, divided	2	tablespoons Dijon mustard
1½	pounds large, uncooked shrimp, peeled and deveined	2	tablespoons chopped fresh dill weed
	salt	2	large cloves garlic, minced
	pepper	¼	cup capers, drained
1	tablespoon grated lemon peel	2	green onions, thinly sliced
3	tablespoons fresh lemon juice	1	head butter lettuce
			sliced lemon
			fresh dill sprigs

Heat 2 tablespoons oil in a large, heavy skillet over medium-high heat. Sprinkle shrimp with salt and pepper; add shrimp to skillet and sauté for 3 minutes until just opaque in the center. Set aside.

Combine peel, juice, mustard, dill and garlic in a large bowl, whisking until well blended. Whisk in remaining ½ cup of oil. Season to taste with salt and pepper.

Stir in shrimp with accumulated juices, capers and green onion. Cover and refrigerate at least 3 hours up to 1 day.

Arrange lettuce leaves on 8 plates. Top evenly with shrimp mixture, drizzling with liquid, if desired. Garnish with lemon slices and dill sprigs.

★ *poquito mas* ★

Caper- the unopened flower bud of a bush found native in the Mediterranean region. Cured in a white vinegar brine, capers develop a piquant, salty-sour flavor used as a condiment or garnish for foods and should be rinsed before using. Capers are found in a variety of sizes from the tiny, nonpareil variety from France to the large buds from Italy and Spain.

grilled skewered chicken with cilantro-tomatillo dipping sauce

yields 30 appetizers

⅓	cup chopped fresh cilantro		2	tablespoons chopped garlic
¼	cup canola oil		2	tablespoons lime juice
3	tablespoons white wine vinegar		5	boneless chicken breasts (approximately 2 pounds)
3	tablespoons honey-mustard		30	bamboo skewers
2-3	tablespoons chopped jalapeño peppers			cilantro-tomatillo dipping sauce

Combine cilantro, oil, vinegar, honey-mustard, pepper, garlic and lime juice in a large bowl. Cut each chicken breast into 6 lengthwise strips and toss in marinade. Cover and refrigerate at least 30 minutes up to 2 hours.

Soak skewers in water at least 30 minutes to prevent burning; set aside. Prepare barbecue grill. Remove chicken from marinade, discarding marinade. Thread each strip on a bamboo skewer.

Grill over medium heat approximately 7 minutes, turning once or twice, until done but not dry. Arrange skewers on a serving platter with dipping sauce.

cilantro-tomatillo dipping sauce

yields 1½ cups

1	large clove garlic, peeled		½	cup finely chopped fresh or canned tomatillos, husks removed
	salt		½	cup sour cream
	pepper		¼	cup mayonnaise
½	cup loosely packed fresh cilantro		¼	jalapeño pepper, seeded and finely minced

grilled skewered chicken *continued*

Position knife blade in a food processor; add garlic, salt and pepper. Process until finely chopped. Add cilantro and process until chopped. Add tomatillo, sour cream and mayonnaise. Process until blended; stir in jalapeño.

★ *poquito mas* ★

Tomatillos- this fruit, called a Mexican green tomato, is a member of the tomato family. It resembles a small green tomato in size, except it has a parchment-like covering called a husk. Choose fruit with tight fitting husks. Before use, remove husk and wash before using. Tomatillos can be used raw in salads or cooked in sauces. Fresh tomatillos can be stored in the refrigerator up to 1 month.

armadillo eggs

yields 2 dozen

½	pound hot bulk sausage	½	cup chopped pecans
1	(8-ounce) package cream cheese, softened	2	(26-ounce) cans mild jalapeño peppers, drained and halved

Brown sausage in a large skillet over medium-high heat, stirring until it crumbles. Drain well.

Combine sausage, cream cheese and pecans in a medium bowl. Spoon mixture into pepper halves. Cover and chill until ready to serve.

picadilla

yields 6 to 8 servings

- 1½ pounds lean ground beef
- 1 (10-ounce) can diced tomatoes with chiles
- ¾ cup chopped onion
- ½ cup chopped red bell pepper
- 2-4 tablespoons chopped jalapeño pepper
- 4 cloves garlic, pressed
- 2 teaspoons sugar
- 2 teaspoons chili powder
- 2 teaspoons dried oregano
- 1 teaspoon onion salt
- ½ teaspoon paprika
- 1 (3-ounce) package slivered almonds

Brown beef in a large skillet over medium-high heat, stirring until it crumbles. Drain well. Stir in tomato, onion, bell pepper, jalapeño pepper, garlic, sugar, chili powder, oregano, onion salt and paprika.

Cook over low heat for 1 hour, stirring often. Stir in almonds. Serve with tortilla chips.

hot crab dip

yields 6 to 8 servings

- 1 (8-ounce) package cream cheese, softened
- 6 ounces crabmeat, drained
- 2 tablespoons finely chopped onion
- 1 tablespoon milk
- ½ teaspoon cream-style horseradish
- ¼ teaspoon salt
- dash pepper
- ⅓ cup sliced almonds, toasted

Preheat oven to 350°. Combine cream cheese, crab, onion, milk, horseradish, salt and pepper in a small bowl. Spoon into a small, lightly greased casserole dish. Sprinkle with toasted almonds.

Bake for 15 minutes or until hot and bubbly. Serve warm with crackers.

gruyère fondue with salsa verde

yields 6 servings

⅓	cup packed fresh basil leaves		3	cups (12 ounces) shredded Gruyère cheese
¼	cup chopped fresh parsley		3	cups (12 ounces) shredded Swiss cheese
¼	cup dry vermouth or white wine		2	tablespoons cornstarch
1	tablespoon Dijon mustard		1½	cups dry white wine
2	cloves garlic, peeled			
	salt			
	pepper			

Combine basil, parsley, vermouth, mustard and garlic in the container of a blender. Puree until smooth. Season to taste with salt and pepper. Cover tightly and let stand at room temperature. (May be prepared 2 hours ahead.)

Combine cheeses and cornstarch in a large bowl, tossing until well blended; set aside.

Heat wine in a large, heavy saucepan over medium heat. Add cheese to wine in 3 batches, whisking after each addition until mixture is melted and smooth. Heat until mixture begins to simmer, stirring constantly. Do not boil. Stir in half of salsa mixture and season to taste with salt and pepper. Spoon remaining salsa mixture on top. Keep fondue very warm for a smooth consistency. Serve with French bread cubes or fresh vegetables.

three cheese baked artichoke dip

yields 12 to 16 servings

2	bags pita or pocket bread	3	cups (12 ounces) shredded mozzarella cheese
2	(6-ounce) jars marinated artichoke hearts, drained	1	(8-ounce) package cream cheese, softened
⅓-½	onion, finely chopped	1	cup freshly grated Parmesan cheese
2-4	cloves garlic, minced	1	cup mayonnaise

Preheat oven to 350°. Cut pita bread in to chip-size triangles and separate into 2 pieces each. Place on a baking sheet and bake for 5 to 7 minutes or until crispy.

Position knife blade in food processor; add artichoke, onion and garlic. Process until chopped.

Transfer mixture to a large bowl. Stir in cheeses and mayonnaise. Spoon into a lightly greased 2-quart casserole dish. Bake for 30 minutes or until lightly browned and bubbly. Serve hot with pita chips.

For extra flavor, brush pita chips with olive oil and sprinkle with Italian seasoning before baking.

brie en croûte

yields 6 to 8 servings

1	large egg	½	cup raspberry preserves or jam of choice
1	tablespoon water	¼	cup toasted almonds, optional
1	sheet frozen puff pastry, thawed	1	(7-ounce) wheel Brie cheese

Preheat oven to 400°. Combine egg and water; set aside. Unfold puff pastry on a lightly floured surface. Roll into a 12-inch square. Cut corners to make a circle.

Spread preserves in center of pastry to the same size as cheese. Sprinkle with almonds, if desired. Place cheese over almonds.

Brush edges of pastry with egg mixture. Fold two opposite sides over cheese. Trim remaining pastry to 2-inches from edge of cheese. Fold remaining two sides onto pastry, pressing edges to seal.

Place pastry, seam side down, on a greased baking sheet. Decorate top with pastry scraps; brush top and sides with remaining egg mixture.

Bake for 20 minutes or until golden brown. Let stand 5 minutes before serving. Serve with crackers.

artichoke bread

yields 12 servings

¼	cup butter or margarine	1	cup (4 ounces) shredded Monterey Jack cheese
2-3	cloves garlic, pressed	1	cup freshly grated Parmesan cheese
2	teaspoons sesame seeds	½	cup sour cream
1	(14-ounce) can artichoke hearts, drained and chopped	1	(16-ounce) loaf French bread
		½	cup shredded cheddar cheese

Preheat oven to 350°. Melt butter in a skillet over medium-high heat. Add garlic and sesame seeds; sauté until lightly browned. Remove from heat and stir in artichoke, Monterey Jack cheese, Parmesan cheese and sour cream.

Cut bread in half lengthwise. Scoop out center of each piece, leaving a 1-inch shell. Add approximately ½ of the removed bread pieces to the artichoke mixture, stirring until blended. Spoon artichoke mixture into shells and sprinkle with cheddar cheese.

Place on a baking sheet and cover with foil. Bake for 25 minutes. Remove foil and bake 5 minutes. Cool slightly and cut into slices.

spinach-feta bread

yields 16 servings

1	cup (4 ounces) crumbled feta cheese	1	(10-ounce) package frozen chopped spinach, thawed and well drained
1	(3-ounce) package cream cheese, softened		
½	teaspoon dried oregano	4	cloves garlic, minced
¼	teaspoon salt	1	large egg
1	(14-ounce) can artichoke hearts, well drained and chopped	1	(16-ounce) loaf frozen white bread dough, thawed
			vegetable cooking spray
		2	tablespoons grated Parmesan cheese

Preheat oven to 350°. Combine feta, cream cheese, oregano, salt, artichoke, spinach, garlic and egg in a large bowl, stirring until well blended.

Roll dough into a 16 x 10-inch rectangle on a lightly floured surface. Spread spinach mixture over the dough, leaving a ½-inch border around sides. Roll up dough, jelly roll fashion, starting with the long side. Pinch seam and ends to seal.

Place roll, seam side down, on a baking sheet sprayed with cooking spray. Cut diagonal slits into the top of the roll using a sharp knife. Cover and let rise in a warm place for 1 hour or until doubled in size.

Sprinkle Parmesan cheese over the top of the roll. Bake for 45 minutes or until golden brown.

mushroom croustades

yields 24 appetizers

24	slices firm-textured white bread		1	tablespoon chopped fresh parsley
¼	cup butter		½	teaspoon lemon juice
3	tablespoons chopped shallots or onion		¼	teaspoon salt
1	(8-ounce) package mushrooms, finely chopped		⅛	teaspoon cayenne pepper
				dash black pepper
2	tablespoons all-purpose flour		2	tablespoons grated Parmesan cheese
1	cup heavy whipping cream			sour cream, optional
2	tablespoons chopped fresh chives			chopped chives, optional

Preheat oven to 400°. Cut a circle with a 3-inch round cutter from each slice of bread, discarding crusts. Press each bread round carefully into a lightly greased muffin cup. Bake until golden brown; set aside.

Melt butter in a medium saucepan over medium heat. Add shallots and sauté for 5 minutes. Stir in mushrooms and cook, uncovered, for 15 minutes or until most of the liquid evaporates.

Add flour, stirring until well blended. Cook 1 minute, stirring constantly. Gradually add cream; cook over medium heat, stirring constantly, until mixture is thickened and bubbly. Cook 1 minute more; remove from heat. Stir in chives, parsley, lemon juice, salt, cayenne and black pepper.

Place bread cups on an ungreased baking sheet. Spoon filling into cups and sprinkle with Parmesan.

Reduce oven temperature to 350° and bake for 15 minutes. Top with sour cream and chives, if desired.

party sandwiches

yields 12 sandwiches

1	(12-count) package Hawaiian rolls or rolls of your choice	½	teaspoon Worcestershire sauce
12	slices ham	½	tablespoon poppy seeds
12	slices Swiss cheese	1 ½	tablespoons yellow mustard
½	cup butter, melted	1	tablespoon dried minced onion

Cut rolls in half and layer ham and cheese in center. Place in a 13 x 9-inch baking pan.

Combine butter, Worcestershire sauce, poppy seeds, mustard and onion in a small bowl; pour over sandwiches. Cover with foil and refrigerate 8 hours or overnight.

Preheat oven to 350°. Bake, covered, for 10 minutes. Uncover, and bake 5 to 10 minutes.

Recipe may be easily doubled.

mushroom-cheese toast

yields 12 servings

½	cup butter, softened	1	(8-ounce) package mushrooms, finely chopped
¾	cup mayonnaise	8	green onions (tops only), finely chopped
3	cups (12 ounces) shredded mozzarella cheese	1	(4.25-ounce) can chopped ripe olives
		1	loaf Italian or French bread

Preheat oven to 350°. Combine butter and mayonnaise in a large bowl, stirring until blended. Stir in cheese, mushroom, onion and olives.

Slice bread lengthwise in half. Spread mushroom mixture on each half and wrap individually in foil.

Bake for 20 minutes; remove foil.

Broil 5 to 7 inches away from heat until bubbly. Slice and serve.

artichokes with tres sauces

yields 1 per person

fresh artichokes   **lemon juice**

Wash artichokes well to remove sand and dirt trapped within leaves. Cut off stems with scissors or a sharp knife. Cut one-fourth off the top of artichoke. Snap off the tough bottom row of leaves by bending them back from the core.

Place artichokes, top side down, in 1 to 2 inches of boiling water. Add 1½ teaspoons of lemon juice to the water to avoid discoloration. Cover and steam for 45 minutes or until tender. Drain and serve hot or chilled with sauces.

To eat the artichoke, tear off the leaves, dip in sauce, scraping the fleshy meat off the leaf between your teeth and discard the tough part of the leaf. Do not eat the small spiny centers of the artichoke. Scoop spines away from heart with a spoon and discard. Artichoke hearts and bottom may be diced and eaten.

artichoke sauces
blanca butter sauce
yields 1⅔ cups

¼	cup Chablis or dry white wine	⅓	cup half-and-half
¼	cup white wine vinegar	1½	cups butter, softened
3	shallots, minced		

Combine wine, vinegar and shallots in a medium saucepan over medium-high heat. Bring mixture to a boil; reduce heat and simmer 8 minutes or until reduced to ⅓ cup.

Stir in half-and-half; simmer 8 minutes, stirring frequently. Remove from heat.

Add butter, stirring until smooth. Serve immediately.

artichoke sauces *continued*

creamy citrus mayonnaise
yields approximately 1 cup

¾ cup mayonnaise
2 tablespoons frozen orange juice concentrate, thawed

1 tablespoon lemon juice
¼-½ teaspoon lemon-pepper seasoning

Combine mayonnaise, undiluted orange juice concentrate, lemon juice and lemon-pepper seasoning in a small bowl. Cover and refrigerate at least 2 hours.

easy dilled hollandaise sauce
yields 1¼ cups

⅓ cup butter or margarine
1 (1.25-ounce) envelope hollandaise sauce mix
1 cup milk

1 tablespoon fresh dill weed or 1 teaspoon dried
½ teaspoon grated lemon peel
1 tablespoon lemon juice

Melt butter in a small saucepan over low heat. Add sauce mix, whisking mixture until well blended. Gradually add milk, whisking until smooth.

Bring mixture to a boil over medium-high heat, stirring constantly. Reduce heat and simmer 1 minute. Stir in dill, lemon peel and juice. Serve warm.

crab-artichoke tarts

yields 32 appetizers

1	(4-ounce) carton egg substitute	1	(6-ounce) can crabmeat, drained and flaked
2	teaspoons all-purpose flour		vegetable cooking spray
⅛	teaspoon dried thyme	32	won ton wrappers
¼	teaspoon salt	3	tablespoons grated Parmesan cheese
⅛	teaspoon black pepper	2	tablespoons chopped green onion
⅓	cup bottled roasted red bell peppers, drained and chopped	1	tablespoon butter, melted
1	(14-ounce) can artichoke hearts, drained and chopped		

Preheat oven to 350°. Combine egg, flour, thyme salt and pepper in a bowl. Add bell pepper, artichoke and crabmeat, stirring well.

Coat 32 miniature muffin cups with cooking spray. Gently press 1 won ton wrapper into each muffin cup, allowing ends to extend above edges of cups.

Spoon crab mixture into each cup and sprinkle with cheese and green onion. Brush edges of cups with melted butter.

Bake for 20 minutes or until crab mixture is set and edges of won ton wrappers are golden brown.

spinach stuffed mushrooms

yields 12 to 16 appetizers

12-16 large mushrooms
½   (12-ounce) package frozen spinach soufflé, thawed
½   cup dry bread crumbs
1   teaspoon lemon juice

½   teaspoon dried minced onion or ¼ cup chopped red onion
¼   teaspoon salt
¼   cup grated Parmesan cheese

Preheat oven to 350°. Remove stems from mushrooms and place caps on a lightly greased baking sheet. Finely chop stems and place in a medium bowl.

Add soufflé, bread crumbs, lemon juice, onion and salt, stirring until well blended. Spoon spinach mixture into caps and sprinkle evenly with cheese.

Bake for 20 minutes.

jalapeño pepper pie

yields 4 to 6 servings

½   cup sliced jalapeño peppers
4   cups (16 ounces) shredded cheddar cheese

6   large eggs, lightly beaten

Preheat oven to 350°. Place pepper slices in the bottom of a greased 8 x 8-inch baking dish. Sprinkle evenly with cheese. Pour eggs over cheese.

Bake for 30 to 35 minutes or until a knife inserted in the center comes out clean. Cut into bite-size squares.

pepper poppers

yields approximately 2 dozen

1	(8-ounce) package cream cheese, softened
1	cup (4 ounces) shredded sharp cheddar cheese
1	cup (4 ounces) shredded Monterey Jack cheese
6	strips bacon, cooked and crumbled
¼	teaspoon salt
¼	teaspoon garlic powder
¼	teaspoon chili powder
1	pound fresh jalapeño peppers, halved lengthwise and seeded
½	cup dry bread crumbs

Preheat oven to 300°. Combine cheeses, bacon, salt, garlic powder and chili powder in a large bowl, mixing well.

Spoon approximately 2 tablespoons into each pepper half. Roll in bread crumbs and place in a greased 15 x 10-inch baking pan. Bake, uncovered, for 20 minutes for a spicy flavor, 30 minutes for medium and 40 minutes for mild.

★ *poquito mas* ★

When cutting or seeding hot peppers, use rubber or plastic gloves to protect your hands. Avoid touching your face or eyes.

sausages with sweet and sour figs

yields approximately 40 appetizers

1	cup sugar		1	tablespoon olive oil
1	cup red wine vinegar		¼	cup white wine, divided
1	stick cinnamon		¼	cup water
4	whole cloves		2	teaspoons tomato sauce
1	slice lemon			salt
1	pound fresh small figs or dried figs			freshly ground pepper
1½	pounds lean breakfast or Italian sweet sausage links			

Combine sugar, vinegar, cinnamon, cloves and lemon in a large saucepan over medium-high heat. Bring mixture to a boil; reduce heat and simmer 5 minutes. Add figs; cover and simmer for 20 minutes. Let figs cool in syrup. Cover and let stand at room temperature 8 hours or overnight.

Heat oil and 2 tablespoons white wine in a medium skillet over low heat. Add sausages and cook until wine evaporates and sausages are cooked and brown. Remove sausages from skillet; set aside.

Pour off most of the fat from the skillet. Add water and remaining 2 tablespoons of wine. Cook over medium-high heat, stirring to loosen browned bits on the bottom of the pan. Add tomato sauce, salt and pepper, stirring until well blended; set aside.

Drain figs, discarding syrup. Add figs and sausages to skillet. Cover and cook over medium heat until well heated. To serve, cut figs in halves or quarters. Cut sausages into 3 to 4 slices. Place a piece of sausage and a piece of fig on a toothpick and transfer to a serving dish. Pour sauce over sausages and figs. Serve immediately.

This recipe may be assembled in advance, covered and reheated until ready to serve. These tapas (appetizers) are usually served with cocktails or apéritifs. Try them with a chilled bottle of Chardonnay.

blue cheese and brie quesadillas with pear and brown sugar compote

yields 32 appetizers

	vegetable oil	8	ounces Brie cheese, rind removed and thinly sliced
16	small flour tortillas		pear and brown sugar compote
8	ounces crumbled blue cheese		

Heat a small amount of oil in a large skillet over medium-high heat. Place 1 tortilla in the skillet and sprinkle with 1 ounce each of blue cheese and Brie. Cover with another tortilla and cook 1 to 2 minutes until golden brown. Carefully turn quesadilla over and cook 1 minute or until golden brown and cheese melts. Repeat with remaining tortillas and cheese.

Cut quesadillas into quarters and serve immediately with compote.

pear and brown sugar compote

1	tablespoon butter	¼	teaspoon ground cinnamon
¼	cup firmly packed light brown sugar		pinch salt
1	pound pears, peeled and finely diced	1	tablespoon water
		1	tablespoon cornstarch

Heat butter in a saucepan over medium heat. Add brown sugar, pears, cinnamon and salt. Cook, stirring frequently, until pears are soft.

Combine water and cornstarch; stir into pear mixture. Cook over medium-high heat until mixture boils; boil 1 minute. Remove from heat.

chicken and mushroom quesadillas

yields 32 appetizers

¼	cup butter	⅔	cup finely chopped onion
2½	teaspoons chili powder	⅓	cup chopped fresh cilantro
2	cloves garlic, minced	2½	cups (10 ounces) shredded Monterey Jack cheese
1	teaspoon dried oregano		salt
4	ounces mushrooms, sliced		pepper
4	ounces shiitake mushrooms, stems removed and sliced		olive oil
1½	cups shredded cooked chicken	16	flour tortillas

Melt butter in a large skillet over medium-high heat. Add chili powder, garlic and oregano; sauté 1 minute or until fragrant. Add mushrooms and sauté 10 minutes or until tender. Remove from heat.

Stir in chicken, onion and cilantro; cool 10 minutes. Stir in cheese and season to taste with salt and pepper. Cover and refrigerate up to 8 hours.

Prepare barbecue grill. Brush oil lightly on 1 side of 8 tortillas. Place tortillas, oil side down, on a large baking sheet. Spoon chicken mixture evenly on tortillas and top with remaining 8 tortillas, pressing down lightly. Brush tops with oil.

Grill quesadillas approximately 3 minutes per side or until thoroughly heated and golden brown. Cut into quarters and serve with salsa and sour cream.

buffalo chicken wings

yields 6 appetizer servings or 4 main dish servings

4	stalks celery		3-4	tablespoons hot sauce
3	pounds (12 to 14) chicken wings		1½	tablespoons cider vinegar
6	cups vegetable oil			salt
¼	cup unsalted butter			blue cheese dressing, optional

Cut celery into thin sticks and soak in a bowl of ice water at least 30 minutes up to an hour, until ready to serve.

Cut off chicken wing tips and cut wings in half at the joint.

Heat oil to 380° in a large, 5- to 6-quart, deep heavy pan. Just before oil reaches 380°, pat dry 6 or 7 wings. Carefully lower wings into hot oil and fry, stirring occasionally, for 5 to 8 minutes or until thoroughly cooked, golden brown and crisp. Drain on paper towels. Repeat with remaining wings, patting dry before frying and allowing oil to return to 380°.

Melt butter in a skillet over medium-low heat. Stir in hot sauce and vinegar; season to taste with salt. Add cooked wings, tossing to coat. Serve hot or at room temperature with dressing and celery sticks.

Easily doubled.

sweet and sour chicken wings

yields 8 to 10 servings

3	pounds chicken wings		1	chicken bouillon cube
	salt		¼	cup ketchup
2-3	large eggs, lightly beaten		½	cup sugar
	cornstarch		½	cup vinegar
	vegetable oil		1	tablespoon soy sauce
½	cup hot water			

Cut off chicken wing tips and cut wings in half at the joint; sprinkle with salt. Dip wings in egg and dredge in cornstarch.

Pour oil to a depth of 2-inches in a large, heavy skillet; heat to 375°. Fry wings in batches without crowding 8 to 10 minutes or until thoroughly cooked, golden brown and crisp. Drain on paper towels. Arrange wings in a single layer in a large, shallow pan; set aside.

Preheat oven to 325°. Combine water and bouillon in a small bowl, stirring until bouillon dissolves. Stir in ketchup, vinegar, sugar and soy sauce. Pour sauce over wings. Cover with foil and bake for 45 minutes. Uncover and bake 15 minutes.

Recipe easily doubled.

wonderful iced tea

yields 4 to 5 quarts

5	family-size tea bags		1	(6-ounce) can frozen limeade concentrate, undiluted
2	cups boiling water		1½	tablespoons vanilla extract
3	quarts cold water		1½	tablespoons almond extract
2	cup sugar			fresh mint leaves
1	(6-ounce) can frozen lemonade concentrate, undiluted			lime slices

Place tea bags in a large pitcher or gallon jug; add boiling water. Set aside and steep 10 to 15 minutes.

Combine water and sugar in a large saucepan over medium-high heat. Bring mixture to a boil; boil until sugar dissolves. Remove from heat.

Remove tea bags from pitcher and add sugar water, lemonade, limeade and extracts, stirring well. Cover and refrigerate at least 4 hours or overnight. Serve over ice and garnish glasses with mint and lime slices.

lemon-pineapple tea

yields approximately 1 gallon

6	cups brewed tea		4	cups water
1	cup sugar		2½	cups pineapple juice
1	(6-ounce) can frozen lemonade concentrate, undiluted			

Combine tea and sugar in a large plastic pitcher, stirring until sugar dissolves. Stir in lemonade, water and juice. Cover and freeze, stirring occasionally, until almost frozen. Serve slushy.

citrus-mint tea cooler

yields 1 quart

3	small tea bags		2	cups water
2	tablespoons fresh mint		⅔	cup fresh grapefruit juice
1	cup boiling water		½	cup lemon juice
⅔	cup sugar			fresh mint leaves

Place tea bags and mint in a 2-cup measuring cup and add boiling water. Cover and steep for 5 minutes. Pour mixture into a pitcher, discarding tea bags and mint.

Add sugar, stirring until it dissolves. Stir in water and juices. Serve over ice and garnish glasses with mint. Easily doubled.

spiced tea punch

yields 1 gallon

2	quarts water		2	cups sugar
1	teaspoon allspice		1	(46-ounce) can pineapple juice
½	teaspoon whole cloves		2	(6-ounce) cans frozen orange juice concentrate, undiluted
½	teaspoon nutmeg			
2	sticks cinnamon		2	(6-ounce) cans frozen lemonade concentrate, undiluted
½	cup tea leaves or 4 family size tea bags			

Bring water to a boil in a large pot. Place allspice, cloves, nutmeg and cinnamon in a small piece of cloth and secure with string. Place spice bag in water and boil for 5 minutes; remove from heat. Add tea leaves or bags; steep 10 to 15 minutes and strain.

Add sugar, juices and lemonade, stirring until sugar dissolves. Pour into a large container; cover and refrigerate until chilled.

junior league punch

yields approximately 1½ gallons

2	cups boiling water		1	(46-ounce) can unsweetened pineapple juice
1	(6-ounce) package any flavor gelatin		1	gallon water
1	(12-ounce) can frozen lemonade concentrate, undiluted		1	tablespoon almond extract
1	cup sugar		1	(1-liter) bottle ginger ale

Combine boiling water and gelatin in a large plastic container, stirring until gelatin dissolves. Stir in lemonade and sugar, stirring well.

Add pineapple juice, water and extract. Cover and freeze a day before serving. Remove punch from freezer 6 to 8 hours before serving (if frozen solid). Stir in ginger ale just before serving. Punch may be refrozen if ginger ale has not been added.

★ *poquito mas* ★

To keep beverages from diluting, make ice cubes from ginger ale or flavored water. For a special surprise, immerse a cherry into each cube.

ruby red sangría

yields 8 servings

⅓	cup fresh orange juice	¼	cup Cointreau or other orange-flavored liqueur
3	tablespoons fresh lemon juice	1	quart red wine
2	tablespoons powdered sugar	1-1¼	cups club soda
½	cup brandy		thinly sliced oranges and lemons

Combine juices and sugar in a large glass pitcher. Stir in brandy, liqueur and 8 ice cubes. Add red wine and club soda, stirring until well chilled.

Pour into chilled glasses and garnish with orange and lemon slices.

cerveza margaritas

yields approximately 1 quart

1	(12-ounce) bottle of Corona Beer	12	ounces tequila
1	(12-ounce) can frozen limeade concentrate, undiluted		margarita salt
1	(12-ounce) can lemon-lime carbonated beverage		lime wedges

Combine beer, limeade, lemon-lime carbonated beverage and tequila in a large container. Cover and refrigerate until well chilled.

Dip rim of glasses in water or lime juice, then margarita salt. Serve margaritas over ice in salted glasses. Garnish with lime wedges.

margaritas

yields 1 gallon

1	liter tequila
1/3	liter Triple Sec or other orange-flavored liqueur
2	cups Lasco lemon mix

1/2	cup Rose's lime juice
	margarita salt
	fresh lime wedges

Combine tequila, liqueur, lemon mix and lime juice in a large, 1-gallon container. Cover and shake until mix dissolves. Add enough cold water to make 1 gallon; shake well. Refrigerate at least 4 hours or overnight.

Dip rim of glasses in water or lime juice, then margarita salt. Serve margaritas over ice in salted glasses. Garnish with lime wedges.

Variations: For frozen margaritas, freeze mixture until slushy.

For strawberry margaritas, pour 1 quart margarita mixture into the container of a blender. Add several frozen strawberries and a few ice cubes. Blend until slushy.

Lasco Lemon Mix is a powdered bartending mix and can be found at liquor stores.

★ *poquito mas* ★

Mexican limes- this lime ranges from green to bright yellow outside, with a solid lemon color inside. Much smaller than the usual lime, it is juicier and more aromatic. If you can find these limes, buy them. They taste better and cost less. Tip: try these in your next margarita!

south of the border bloody mary

yields 10 servings

1¼ teaspoons salt	¼ cup salsa or picante
1 teaspoon onion powder	½ teaspoon hot sauce
⅛ teaspoon garlic powder	dash Worcestershire sauce
1 (48-ounce) can tomato-vegetable juice cocktail	15 ounces vodka
¼ cup lime juice	celery sticks

Combine salt, onion powder and garlic powder in a large pitcher. Stir in a small amount of tomato-vegetable juice to dissolve.

Add remaining tomato-vegetable juice, lime juice, salsa, hot sauce and Worcestershire sauce, stirring until well blended.

Fill each glass with ice and 1½ ounces of vodka. Fill with juice mixture and garnish with celery sticks.

minted vodka lemonade

yields 4 to 6 servings

1 cup packed, chopped fresh mint leaves	1 cup fresh lemon juice
⅔ cup sugar	crushed ice
1½ cups vodka	fresh mint sprigs

Combine mint and sugar in a large bowl. Stir in vodka and lemon juice. Cover and refrigerate for 2 hours. Strain mixture into a large pitcher.

Fill glasses with crushed ice. Pour lemonade mixture over ice and garnish with mint sprigs.

bourbon slush

yields approximately 3 quarts

2 cups boiling water	1 cup bourbon
2 family-size tea bags	1 (6-ounce) can frozen orange juice concentrate, undiluted
½ cup sugar	1 (6-ounce) can frozen lemonade concentrate, undiluted
7 cups cold water	
1 cup vodka	

Combine boiling water and tea bags in a large plastic container; steep for 30 minutes. Discard tea bags and add sugar, stirring until it dissolves. Stir in water, vodka, bourbon, orange juice and lemonade.

Cover and freeze 8 hours or overnight, stirring occasionally.

gin fizz

yields 4 servings

1   (6-ounce) can frozen limeade
    concentrate, undiluted
6   ounces (¾ cup) milk

6   ounces (¾ cup) gin
    dash orange flower water
    club soda

Combine limeade, milk, gin and orange flower water in the container of a blender. Add ice cubes; blend until slushy, adding more ice cubes if necessary.

Fill glasses ⅔ to ¾ full and top with club soda.

Use the empty limeade can to measure milk and gin.

champagne punch

yields approximately 2 quarts

2   cups orange juice
1   (10-ounce) package frozen sliced
    strawberries, thawed and
    undrained

1   bottle champagne
    fresh strawberries

Combine orange juice and strawberries in the container of a blender. Blend until smooth. Combine strawberry mixture and champagne in a large pitcher.

Serve immediately and garnish glasses with strawberries.

sunshine slush

yields approximately 1 gallon

3   cups water
1   cup sugar
2   medium ripe bananas, sliced
2   (12-ounce) cans pineapple juice
1   (6-ounce) can frozen orange juice
     concentrate, undiluted

1   (6-ounce) can frozen lemonade
     concentrate, undiluted
2   tablespoons lemon juice
2   cups vodka or light rum
     ginger ale or carbonated lemon-lime
     beverage

Combine water and sugar in a saucepan over medium-high heat, stirring until sugar dissolves. Bring to a boil; reduce heat and simmer for 3 minutes. Let cool. Pour into one-gallon container.

Combine bananas and half of the pineapple juice in the container of a blender. Blend until smooth. Stir into cooled sugar syrup. Add remaining pineapple juice, orange juice, lemonade, lemon juice and vodka.

Cover and store mixture in the freezer. To serve, combine equal amounts of slush and ginger ale or carbonated lemon-lime beverage.

Excellent and refreshing. Best made in a container with a wide opening.

Breakfast

and

Breads

corn tortilla quiche

yields 6 servings

1	pound bulk pork sausage		1	(4-ounce) can diced green chiles
	vegetable oil		6	large eggs, lightly beaten
5	corn tortillas		½	cup heavy whipping cream
1	cup (4 ounces) shredded Monterey Jack cheese		½	cup small-curd cottage cheese
1	cup (4 ounces) shredded cheddar cheese		½	teaspoon chili powder
			¼	cup minced fresh cilantro

Preheat oven to 350°. Brown sausage in a large skillet over medium-high heat, stirring until it crumbles. Drain well; transfer to a plate and set aside.

Heat a small amount of oil in the skillet over medium heat. Quickly dip each tortilla in oil to soften and drain on paper towels. Place tortillas in a greased 9-inch pie plate, overlapping to cover entire pie plate and extending ½-inch over the rim.

Layer Monterey Jack, cheddar cheese and chiles in pie shell. Combine eggs, cream, cottage cheese, chili powder and cilantro and pour over chiles.

Bake for 45 minutes or until the center is set and puffed. Cut into wedges and garnish with cilantro.

migas

yields 4 to 6 servings

2	tablespoons vegetable oil		8	large eggs, lightly beaten
1	onion, chopped		6	corn tortillas, torn into pieces
1	green bell pepper, chopped			salt
2-3	jalapeño peppers, seeded and chopped			pepper
				salsa, optional

Heat oil in a medium skillet over medium-high heat. Add onion, bell pepper and jalapeño pepper; sauté until tender.

Add eggs and cook, stirring and folding over to form soft curds. Just before eggs are done, fold in tortillas. Cook until desired degree of doneness. Serve with salsa, if desired.

★ poquito mas ★

Migas are scrambled eggs combined with pieces of corn tortillas and are usually served for breakfast.

spinach sausage brunch casserole

yields 8 to 10 servings

1	pound bulk Italian sausage
1	cup chopped onion
1	(7-ounce) jar roasted red bell peppers, drained, chopped and divided or 1 large red bell pepper, roasted, chopped and divided
1	(10-ounce) package frozen chopped spinach, thawed and well drained

1	cup all-purpose flour
¼	cup Parmesan cheese
1	tablespoon chopped fresh basil or 1 teaspoon dried
½	teaspoon salt
8	large eggs
2	cups milk
1	cup (4 ounces) shredded provolone cheese

Preheat oven to 425°. Brown sausage and onion in a large skillet over medium-high heat, stirring until it crumbles. Drain on paper towels. Place sausage mixture in a greased 13 x 9-inch baking dish. Arrange half of roasted pepper over sausage and top with spinach.

Combine flour, Parmesan cheese, basil and salt in a large bowl; set aside. Combine eggs and milk, beating until well blended. Add egg mixture to flour mixture, beating until smooth. Pour milk mixture over spinach.

Bake for 20 to 25 minutes or until a knife inserted in the center comes out clean. Sprinkle casserole with remaining roasted pepper and provolone cheese. Bake for 1 to 2 minutes or until cheese melts. Let stand 5 minutes; cut into squares.

eggs olé

yields 6 to 8 servings

1   pound bulk sausage
¼   cup butter
1   green bell pepper, chopped
5   green onions, chopped
1   (16-ounce) package process cheese spread, cut into pieces
12   large eggs, lightly beaten

1   (10-ounce) can diced tomatoes with chiles, drained
1   (8-ounce) container sour cream
1   (4-ounce) can sliced mushrooms or 1 pound fresh sliced
1   cup chopped green chiles

Preheat oven to 325°. Brown sausage in a large skillet over medium-high heat, stirring until it crumbles. Drain; transfer to a plate and set aside.

Melt butter in skillet over medium-high heat. Add bell pepper and onion; sauté until tender. Reduce heat to low. Add cheese spread, stirring until it melts.

Combine eggs, tomato, sour cream, mushroom and green chiles in a large bowl. Add reserved sausage and cheese mixture, stirring until well blended. Spoon into a greased 13 x 9-inch baking dish. Bake for 1 hour.

fiesta eggs benedict

yields 4 servings

6	hard-cooked eggs, sliced	½	cup mayonnaise
1	(10¾-ounce) can cheddar cheese soup	8	thick slices ham
1	(4-ounce) can diced green chiles	4	English muffins, halved and lightly toasted
½	cup milk	¼	cup chopped green onions

Preheat oven to 350°. Place sliced eggs in a bowl. Combine soup, chiles, milk and mayonnaise; pour over eggs and set aside.

Brown ham slices on both sides in a nonstick skillet over medium-high heat. Place muffin halves in a single layer on the bottom of a 13 x 9-inch baking dish. Layer ham slices on muffin and top evenly with egg mixture. Sprinkle with green onions and bake 20 minutes. Serve with salsa, if desired.

★ *poquito mas* ★

Hard-cooked eggs- place eggs in a saucepan and cover with cold water, at least 1-inch above eggs. Bring to a boil; reduce heat to just below a simmer. Cook, covered, for 15 to 20 minutes. Cool at once in cold water to prevent a dark surface on the yolk and make it easier to peel.

crème brûlée french toast

yields 8 to 10 servings

½	cup unsalted butter		1½	cups half-and-half
1	cup firmly packed light brown sugar		1	teaspoon vanilla extract
2	tablespoons corn syrup		1	teaspoon Grand Marnier or other orange-flavored liqueur
6	(1-inch) slices country-style bread, crusts removed if desired		¼	teaspoon salt
5	large eggs			

Melt butter in a heavy saucepan over medium heat. Add brown sugar and corn syrup, stirring until well blended. Pour mixture into a 13 x 9-inch baking dish. Arrange bread slices over sugar mixture in a single layer.

Combine eggs, half-and-half, vanilla, liqueur and salt in a bowl, whisking until well blended. Pour over bread. Cover and refrigerate 8 hours or overnight.

Preheat oven to 350°. Uncover french toast and let stand to room temperature. Bake for 30 to 40 minutes or until golden brown.

stuffed french toast

yields 8 to 10 servings

8	(1-inch) slices French bread		1	cup maple syrup
2	(8-ounce) packages cream cheese, cubed		1	tablespoon vanilla extract
			1	teaspoon ground cinnamon
12	large eggs		1	teaspoon ground nutmeg
2	cups milk			dash allspice

Remove crusts from bread and cut into cubes. Place half in the bottom of a lightly greased 13 x 9-inch baking dish. Place cream cheese over bread and top with remaining bread cubes.

Beat eggs in a large bowl until well blended. Beat in milk, syrup, vanilla, cinnamon, nutmeg and allspice. Pour over bread. Cover with plastic wrap and refrigerate 8 hours or overnight.

Preheat oven to 375°. Uncover and let stand until room temperature. Bake for 40 to 45 minutes. Serve with maple syrup.

cottage cheese pancakes

yields 4 servings

6	large eggs		4	tablespoons butter, melted
1	(16-ounce) container cottage cheese		¼	teaspoon ground cinnamon, optional
½	cup flour			

Combine eggs, cottage cheese, flour, butter and cinnamon in the container of a blender. Blend until smooth.

Pour about ¼-cup batter onto a hot, lightly greased griddle or nonstick skillet. Cook pancakes until the tops are covered with bubbles and edges look cooked; turn and cook other side. Serve with jam.

These pancakes are much creamier than regular pancakes. Kids love them!

crunchy granola

yields approximately 6 cups

2	cups old-fashioned oats		¼	teaspoon salt
¾	cup wheat germ		⅔	cup chopped pitted dates
½	cup sliced almonds		⅓	cup dried bananas
½	cup honey		½	cup golden raisins
1	tablespoon vegetable oil		½	cup chopped dried apricots or peaches
1	tablespoon water			
¾	teaspoon ground cinnamon			

Preheat oven to 325°. Combine oats, wheat germ and almonds in a large bowl. Combine honey, oil, water, cinnamon and salt and pour over oats mixture, stirring until well blended. Spread mixture on a lightly greased baking sheet.

Bake for 15 minutes, stirring every 5 minutes; cool. Stir in dates, bananas, raisins and apricots. Store in an airtight container.

spiked fruit

yields 4 to 6 cups

2	large bananas, sliced		½	cup strawberry-banana yogurt
1-2	apples, peeled, cored and chopped		½	cup orange juice
1	tablespoon lemon juice		3	tablespoons light brown sugar
½	cup sliced strawberries		3	tablespoons orange or peach liqueur
¼	cup fresh blueberries			

Combine banana, apple and lemon juice in a large bowl, tossing to coat. Fold in strawberries, blueberries, yogurt, orange juice, brown sugar and liqueur. Cover and refrigerate until chilled. Serve with crunchy granola.

baked pineapple

yields 4 to 6 servings

1	(15.25-ounce) can crushed pineapple, undrained		pinch salt
1	large egg, lightly beaten		butter, melted
½	cup sugar		ground cinnamon
2	tablespoons cornstarch		maraschino cherries

Preheat oven to 325°. Combine pineapple, egg, sugar, cornstarch and salt in a large bowl. Pour into a greased baking dish.

Combine butter and cinnamon; drizzle over pineapple. Garnish with cherries. Bake for 1 hour.

Excellent with ham.

baked fruit

yields 8 servings

1	(15.25-ounce) can sliced peaches, drained	1	(16-ounce) can whole berry cranberry sauce
1	(15.25-ounce) can pineapple chunks, drained	½	cup tapioca

Preheat oven to 350°. Combine peaches, pineapple, cranberry sauce and tapioca in a lightly greased baking dish. Bake for 30 minutes or until hot and bubbly. Serve hot.

tortilla fruit cups

yields 4 servings

4	(6-inch) flour tortillas	¼	cup orange marmalade
1	tablespoon butter or margarine, melted	3	cups fresh chopped fruit such as berries, cantaloupe, kiwi or plums
1	teaspoon sugar	¼	cup chopped pecans, optional
¼	teaspoon ground cinnamon or apple pie spice		

Preheat oven to 350°. Wrap tortillas in foil and bake for 5 to 10 minutes or until warm. Brush both sides of tortillas with butter and place in a 10-ounce custard cup, pleating as necessary to fit.

Combine sugar and cinnamon; sprinkle on inside of tortilla cups. Bake for 10 to 12 minutes or until crisp. Remove tortillas from cups; let cool.

Melt marmalade in a small saucepan over medium-low heat. Combine marmalade and fruit in a large bowl, tossing to coat. Spoon fruit mixture into tortilla cups and sprinkle with pecans, if desired. Serve immediately.

creamy fruit dip
with caramel topping

yields 2 cups

3 (8-ounce) packages cream cheese, softened
1 (10-ounce) jar marshmallow cream
1 tablespoon mayonnaise

1 teaspoon almond extract
   caramel topping
   sliced or slivered almonds, optional

Combine cream cheese, marshmallow cream, mayonnaise and extract in a large bowl, stirring until well blended. Cover and refrigerate 1 hour. Place in a serving container and top with caramel topping and almonds, if desired. Serve with any kind of fruit.

kahlúa fruit dip

yields 3 cups

1 cup heavy whipping cream
1 cup firmly packed light brown sugar
1 cup sour cream

4 teaspoons Kahlúa or other coffee-flavored liqueur
1 teaspoon vanilla extract

Combine cream, sugar, sour cream, liqueur and vanilla in a bowl, whisking until well blended. Cover and refrigerate until ready to serve. Serve with fresh fruit.

Store in an airtight container in the refrigerator up to 2 weeks.

raspberry double cream coffee cake

yields 16 servings

2¼	cups all-purpose flour		½	teaspoon baking soda
¾	cup sugar		½	teaspoon baking powder
¾	cup butter, softened		¼	teaspoon salt
1	large egg			cream cheese filling
1	cup regular, light or nonfat sour cream		1	cup raspberry or other preserves
1	teaspoon almond extract		½	cup sliced almonds

Preheat oven to 350°. Combine flour and sugar in a large mixing bowl. Cut in butter with a pastry blender or fork until mixture resembles a coarse meal. Set aside 1 cup for topping.

Beat egg in a mixing bowl. Stir in sour cream, extract, baking soda, baking powder and salt. Add sour cream mixture to flour mixture, beating at medium speed with an electric mixer until well blended.

Spread batter over bottom and 2-inches up the sides of a greased and floured springform pan.

Spread cream cheese filling over batter to within ½-inch from edge. Spread preserves over cream cheese mixture.

Sprinkle almonds and reserved crumb mixture over the top. Bake for 45 minutes to 1 hour or until cream cheese filling is set and cake is a dark golden brown. Cool 15 minutes in pan on a wire rack. Run knife around sides of cake to loosen; remove sides of pan. Serve warm or cold. Store leftovers, covered, in the refrigerator.

raspberry double cream coffee cake *continued*

cream cheese filling

1   (8-ounce) package cream cheese,   ¼   cup sugar
     softened   1   large egg, lightly beaten

Combine cream cheese, sugar and egg in a small mixing bowl. Beat at medium speed until smooth.

cowboy coffee cake
yields 12 servings

2½   cups all-purpose flour   ½   teaspoon ground cinnamon
2   cups firmly packed light brown sugar ½   teaspoon ground nutmeg
½   teaspoon salt   1   cup buttermilk
⅔   cup shortening   2   large eggs
2   teaspoons baking powder   ½   cup chopped walnuts
½   teaspoon baking soda

Preheat oven to 350°. Combine flour, sugar and salt in a large mixing bowl. Cut in shortening with a pastry blender or fork until mixture resembles a coarse meal. Set aside ½ cup for topping.

Stir baking powder, baking soda, cinnamon and nutmeg into flour mixture.

Combine milk and eggs, beating until well blended. Add milk mixture to flour mixture, stirring until smooth. Pour batter into 2 greased 8-inch cake pans. Sprinkle evenly with reserved crumbs and walnuts. Bake for 15 to 20 minutes or until toothpick inserted in the center comes out clean. Serve hot.

Great for breakfast or dessert.

almond breakfast pizza

yields 4 to 6 servings

crust		almond topping
almond filling	¼	cup sliced almonds, toasted

Preheat oven to 350°. Spread crust dough into an 8-inch circle on a baking sheet or pizza pan. Spread almond filling over crust.

Bake for 1 hour; cool on a wire rack.

Spread almond topping on cooled pastry and sprinkle with almonds. Cut into wedges and serve.

crust

1	cup all-purpose flour	½	cup butter, melted
1	tablespoon water		

Combine flour, water and butter in a small bowl, stirring until well blended.

almond filling

1	cup water	3	large eggs
½	cup butter	½	teaspoon almond extract
1	cup all-purpose flour		

Bring water to a boil in a medium saucepan. Remove from heat and add butter and flour, stirring until well blended. Add eggs, one at a time, beating well after each addition. Stir in almond extract.

almond topping

¼	cup butter, melted	1	teaspoon milk
1½	cups powdered sugar	1	teaspoon almond extract

Combine butter and powdered sugar. Stir in milk and almond extract, adding more powdered sugar, if necessary.

breakfast pastry with fruit preserves

yields 4 to 6 servings

2	cups buttermilk baking mix	¼-½	cup raspberry or strawberry preserves
½	(8-ounce) package cream cheese, softened		icing
¼	cup butter	¼	cup chopped nuts
⅓	cup milk		

Preheat oven to 425°. Place baking mix in a large bowl. Cut cream cheese and butter into baking mix with a pastry blender or fork until mixture resembles a coarse meal. Stir in milk and knead 8 to 10 times, adding more baking mix, if necessary.

Turn out dough onto a lightly greased baking sheet and press into a rectangle. Make 2½-inch cuts at 1-inch intervals along the long sides of the rectangle. Spread raspberry preserves in the center of the dough. Alternately fold the edges over to resemble a braid. Bake for 15 minutes; let cool on a wire rack.

Drizzle icing over cooled pastry and sprinkle with nuts.

icing

1	cup powdered sugar	½	teaspoon vanilla extract
1½	tablespoons milk		

Combine powdered sugar, milk and vanilla in a small bowl, stirring until well blended.

This is a beautiful pastry and so easy. Everyone will think you are a master pastry chef preparing this so early in the morning.

⭐ cream cheese braids

yields four 12-inch loaves

1	cup sour cream	½	cup warm water (105° to 115°)
½	cup sugar	2	eggs, lightly beaten
½	cup butter or margarine, melted	4	cups all-purpose flour
1	teaspoon salt		cream cheese filling
2	(¼-ounce) packages active dry yeast		glaze

Heat sour cream in a small saucepan over low heat. Stir in sugar, butter and salt; cool to lukewarm. Sprinkle yeast over warm water in a large mixing bowl, stirring until yeast dissolves. Add sour cream mixture, eggs and flour, stirring until well blended. Cover tightly and refrigerate 8 hours or overnight.

Divide dough into 4 portions. Roll each portion into a 12 x 8-inch rectangle on a floured surface. Spread one-fourth of the cream cheese filling on each rectangle. Roll up each rectangle jelly roll fashion, starting at the long side. Pinch edges together and slightly fold ends under. Place rolls, seam side down, on greased baking sheets.

Diagonally slice each roll at 2-inch intervals, two-thirds of the way through the dough, alternating on each side to resemble a braid. Cover and let rise in a warm place for 1 hour or until doubled in bulk.

Preheat oven to 375°. Bake for 15 to 20 minutes. Spread glaze over top while still warm.

cream cheese braids *continued*

cream cheese filling
yields approximately 2 cups

2	(8-ounce) packages cream cheese, softened	1	large egg, lightly beaten
¾	cup sugar	2	teaspoons vanilla extract
		⅛	teaspoon salt

Combine cream cheese and sugar in a small mixing bowl or food processor. Stir or process until well blended. Stir in egg, vanilla and salt, mixing well.

glaze
yields 1 cup

2	cups powdered sugar	2	teaspoons vanilla extract
¼	cup milk		

Combine sugar, milk and extract in a small bowl or food processor. Stir or process until well blended.

lime danish pastries

yields 24 servings

6¼-6¾	cups all-purpose flour, divided	1	cup water
1	cup sugar, divided	1	cup milk
2	(¼-ounce) packages active dry yeast	½	cup butter
1½	teaspoons salt	1	large egg

Combine 2 cups flour, ½ cup sugar, yeast and salt in a large bowl; set aside.

Combine water, milk and butter in a saucepan over medium heat. Cook, stirring constantly, until mixture is warm (120° to 130°) and butter is almost melted. Stir milk mixture into flour mixture. Add egg and beat 30 seconds until blended, scraping the sides of the bowl. Beat for 3 minutes, adding as much remaining flour as possible.

Turn dough out onto a lightly floured surface. Knead for 6 to 8 minutes until dough is elastic, adding enough remaining flour to make a moderately stiff dough. Shape into a ball. Place in a greased bowl; cover and let rise for 1 hour or until doubled in bulk.

Punch dough down and turn out onto a floured surface. Divide dough in half; cover and let rest 10 minutes.

Preheat oven to 375°. Roll each piece of dough into a 14 x 9-inch rectangle on a floured surface. Sprinkle each rectangle evenly with remaining ½ cup sugar. Roll, jelly roll fashion, starting at the long side and seal seams. Cut each roll into 12 slices and arrange 2 inches apart on a lightly greased baking sheet. Make indentations on each pastry and fill with a scant tablespoon of filling. Bake for 18 to 20 minutes or until golden brown. Let stand 2 minutes and drizzle with icing. Serve warm.

lime danish pastries *continued*

filling

1   (8-ounce) package cream cheese, softened
½   cup sugar

½   teaspoon grated lime peel
2   tablespoons lime juice

Combine cream cheese, sugar, peel and juice in a bowl, stirring until well blended.

icing

½   cup sifted powdered sugar
1   tablespoon lime juice

1   teaspoon butter, melted

Combine powdered sugar, juice and melted butter, stirring until well blended.

75

sausage cake

yields 12 servings

1	cup raisins		1	teaspoon salt
	boiling water		1	teaspoon baking powder
1	pound bulk pork sausage		1	teaspoon pumpkin pie spice
1½	cups sugar		1	teaspoon baking soda
1½	cups firmly packed light brown sugar		1	cup cold brewed coffee
2	large eggs		1	cup chopped walnuts
3	cups all-purpose flour			

Combine raisins and boiling water to cover in a small bowl; let stand 5 minutes and drain.

Preheat oven to 350°. Beat sausage, sugar and brown sugar in a large mixing bowl at medium speed with an electric mixer until well blended. Add eggs, one at a time, beating until blended after each addition.

Combine flour, salt, baking powder, pumpkin pie spice and baking soda; add to sausage mixture alternately with coffee. Beat at low speed until blended. Stir in raisins and walnuts.

Spoon to a greased Bundt pan and bake for 1½ hours. Cool in pan for 10 minutes; turn out onto a serving platter.

raisin scones

yields 1 dozen

2	cups all-purpose flour	½	cup butter or margarine, cut into pieces
2	tablespoons sugar		
2	teaspoons baking powder	1	cup raisins
½	teaspoon baking soda	¾	cup buttermilk
½	teaspoon salt	1	egg white, lightly beaten
½	teaspoon ground nutmeg		sugar

Preheat oven to 425°. Combine flour, sugar, baking powder, baking soda, salt and nutmeg in a large bowl. Cut in butter with a pastry blender or fork until mixture resembles a coarse meal. Stir raisins and buttermilk into crumb mixture with a fork.

Shape into a ball and knead for 2 minutes on a lightly floured surface. Roll dough to ¾-inch thick. Cut into 3-inch triangles and place on greased baking sheets.

Brush tops with egg white and sprinkle with sugar. Bake for 15 minutes or until golden brown. Serve warm with butter and jam.

nutty apple coconut muffins

yields 1 dozen

1	cup all-purpose flour	¾	cup sugar
1	teaspoon baking soda	¼	cup vegetable oil
1	teaspoon ground cinnamon	2	cups peeled, cored and chopped apples
1	teaspoon ground nutmeg		
½	teaspoon salt	1	cup walnuts or pecans, chopped
1	large egg, lightly beaten	½	cup shredded coconut
			powdered sugar

Preheat oven to 350°. Combine flour, baking soda, cinnamon, nutmeg and salt in a large bowl.

Combine egg, sugar and oil; add to dry ingredients, stirring just until moistened. Fold in apples, nuts and coconut. Spoon batter into a greased muffin pan, filling three-fourths full.

Bake for 30 minutes. Let sit in pan several minutes before turning out. Dust with powdered sugar, if desired.

bran muffins

yields 2 to 3 dozen

3	cups bran flakes	4	large eggs
1	cup all bran cereal	5	cups all-purpose flour
2	cups boiling water	5	teaspoons baking soda
1	cup shortening	1	teaspoon salt
2	cups sugar	1	quart buttermilk

Combine bran flakes and bran cereal in a bowl; pour boiling water over mixture. Let cool.

Preheat oven to 350°. Beat shortening at medium speed in a large bowl with an electric mixer until creamy; gradually add sugar, beating well. Add eggs, one at a time, beating until blended after each addition. Stir in bran mixture.

Combine flour, baking soda and salt; add to shortening mixture alternately with buttermilk, beginning and ending with flour mixture. Beat at low speed until blended after each addition. Spoon batter into a greased muffin pan, filling three-fourths full.

Bake for 18 to 20 minutes. Turn out onto a wire rack to cool.

Uncooked batter stores in refrigerator for 1 week.

⭐ pineapple poppins

yields 1 dozen

2	cups all-purpose flour	¾	cup milk
½	cup sugar	¼	cup butter, melted
1	tablespoon baking powder	¼	cup pineapple juice
½	teaspoon salt	1¼	cups pineapple tidbits
1	large egg, lightly beaten		topping

Preheat oven to 375°. Combine flour, sugar, baking powder and salt in a large bowl.

Combine egg, milk, butter and pineapple juice; add to dry ingredients, stirring just until moistened.

Place paper baking cups in a muffin pan; spoon batter into cups, filling two-thirds full. Top each with 4 or 5 pineapple tidbits.

Sprinkle topping mixture over muffins. Bake for 30 minutes or until toothpick inserted in center comes out clean.

Batter can be baked in mini muffin pans for smaller muffins.

topping

½	cup all-purpose flour	¼	teaspoon ground cinnamon
¼	cup butter, melted	⅓	cup firmly packed light brown sugar

Combine flour and cinnamon in a small bowl. Stir in brown sugar and butter.

sausage muffins

yields 1 dozen

½ **pound bulk sausage**
2 **cups all-purpose flour**
2 **tablespoons sugar**
1 **tablespoon baking powder**
¼ **teaspoon salt**
1 **large egg, lightly beaten**

1 **cup milk**
¼ **cup butter, melted**
¾ **cup (6 ounces) shredded cheddar cheese**
   vegetable cooking spray

Preheat oven to 375°. Brown sausage in a large skillet over medium-high heat, stirring until it crumbles. Drain well and set aside.

Combine flour, sugar, baking powder and salt; make a well in the center.

Combine egg, milk, butter and cheese; add to dry ingredients, stirring just until moistened. Fold in sausage. Spoon batter into a muffin pan coated with cooking spray, filling two-thirds full. Bake for 20 minutes or until golden brown. Remove from pan immediately.

orange-pecan mini muffins

yields 3½ dozen

1	cup butter, softened	1	teaspoon baking soda
1	cup sugar	1	cup buttermilk
2	large eggs	½	cup chopped pecans
2	cups all-purpose flour		vegetable cooking spray
3	tablespoons grated orange peel		topping

Preheat oven to 400°. Beat butter at medium speed with an electric mixer until creamy; gradually add sugar, beating well. Add eggs, one at a time, beating until blended after each addition.

Combine flour, orange peel and baking soda; add to butter mixture alternately with buttermilk, beginning and ending with flour. Fold in pecans. Spoon into mini muffin pans coated with cooking spray, filling almost to the top.

Bake for 20 minutes. Pour topping over muffins. Remove from pans and cool on wire racks.

topping

1	cup firmly packed light brown sugar	⅓	cup fresh orange juice

Combine brown sugar and orange juice in a small bowl.

pumpkin-chocolate chip bread

yields 1 loaf

1⅔	**cups all-purpose flour**
1½	**cups sugar**
2	**teaspoons pumpkin pie spice**
1	**teaspoon baking soda**
½	**teaspoon salt**
¼	**teaspoon baking powder**
2	**large eggs, lightly beaten**

1	**cup canned pumpkin**
½	**cup oil**
⅓	**cup water**
1	**cup semi-sweet chocolate morsels**
½	**cup chopped nuts, optional**
	powdered sugar

Preheat oven to 350°. Combine flour, sugar, spice, baking soda, salt and baking powder in a large bowl.

Combine eggs, pumpkin, oil and water; add to dry ingredients stirring just until moistened. Fold in morsels and nuts. Pour into a greased 9 x 5 x 3-inch loaf pan; level top.

Bake for 1 hour and 15 minutes or until a toothpick inserted near the center comes out clean. Cool in pan 15 minutes. Turn out onto a wire rack; cool completely. Sprinkle with powdered sugar.

Also makes 3 mini loaves; bake 30 to 40 minutes.

peanut butter 'n' banana bread

yields 2 loaves

2½	cups all-purpose flour	¾	cup chunky peanut butter
½	cup sugar	3	tablespoons vegetable oil
½	cup firmly packed light brown sugar	1	teaspoon vanilla extract
1	tablespoon baking powder	1	cup (6 ounces) semi-sweet chocolate morsels
¾	teaspoon salt		peanut butter frosting
¼	teaspoon ground cinnamon		crushed peanuts
3	ripe bananas, mashed		miniature chocolate morsels
1	large egg, lightly beaten		
1	cup milk		

Preheat oven to 350°. Combine flour, sugar, brown sugar, baking powder, salt and cinnamon in a large bowl.

Combine banana, egg, milk, peanut butter, oil and vanilla; add to dry ingredients, stirring just until moistened. Spoon batter into two greased 8 x 4 x 2-inch loaf pans.

Bake for 50 to 55 minutes or until a toothpick inserted near the center comes out clean. Remove from pans; cool on wire rack. Wrap and refrigerate 8 hours or overnight. To serve, frost with peanut butter frosting and garnish with crushed peanuts and miniature chocolate morsels.

peanut butter frosting

yields ½ cup

3	tablespoons chunky peanut butter	1	tablespoon milk
2	tablespoons butter	1	teaspoon vanilla extract
1	cup powdered sugar		

Heat peanut butter and butter in a small saucepan over medium heat, stirring until melted. Remove from heat and stir in sugar, milk and vanilla; add more milk, if necessary, until desired spreading consistency.

oatmeal praline bread

yields 2 loaves

2	cups water	1½	teaspoons baking soda
¾	cup butter	¾	teaspoon salt
1½	cups quick oats	3	large eggs, lightly beaten
2¼	cups all-purpose flour	½	teaspoon vanilla extract
1	cup plus 2 tablespoons sugar		topping
1	cup plus 2 tablespoons firmly packed light brown sugar		

Preheat oven to 350°. Bring water to a boil in a medium saucepan. Remove from heat and stir in butter and oats. Cover and let stand 5 minutes, stirring occasionally, until butter melts.

Combine flour, sugar, brown sugar, soda and salt in a large bowl.

Combine eggs and vanilla; add to dry ingredients, stirring just until moistened. Fold in oat mixture. Spoon batter into two lightly greased 8 x 4-inch loaf pans or one lightly greased Bundt pan.

Bake for 30 to 40 minutes. The top center will be soft; insert a toothpick from the side into the center to test. Cool in pans for 10 minutes.

Pour topping over loaves; let cool in pans. For a Bundt cake, turn out cake over wax paper after baking. Spoon topping over cake, spreading any dripping topping back over top. Topping will harden as it cools.

topping

½	cup butter	2	tablespoons milk
1	cup firmly packed light brown sugar	¾	cup chopped nuts

Combine butter, brown sugar and milk in a saucepan over medium-high heat. Bring mixture to a boil; boil 1 minute. Stir in nuts.

easy batter rolls

yields 1½ dozen

3	cups all-purpose flour, divided	¼	cup vegetable oil
1	(¼-ounce) package active dry yeast	¼	cup honey
1	teaspoon salt	1	large egg
1	cup hot water (120° to 130°)		

Combine 2 cups flour, yeast and salt in a large mixing bowl. Add water, oil, honey and egg; beat for 2 minutes on medium speed with an electric mixer. Beat in remaining 1 cup flour with a wooden spoon. Cover and let rise 1 hour or until double in bulk (dough will be very sticky).

Spoon dough into greased muffin pans, filling one-half full. Let rise 1 hour or until double in bulk.

Preheat oven to 400°. Bake for 10 to 12 minutes or until golden brown.

ever-ready rye biscuits

yields 2 dozen

4   cups self-rising flour, divided
1   cup rye flour, sifted
2   (¼-ounce) packages active dry yeast

2   cups buttermilk
1   cup vegetable oil
2   tablespoons sugar, optional

Preheat oven to 425°. Combine 1 cup self-rising flour, rye flour and yeast in a large bowl.

Combine buttermilk, oil and sugar, if desired; add 2 cups self-rising flour, stirring until well blended. Gradually add yeast mixture, mixing well.

Stir in remaining 1 cup self-rising flour to make a stiff dough (if dough is too stiff, stir in a small amount of water).

Turn out onto a floured surface and knead lightly. Roll to ½-inch thickness and cut with a 2-inch round cutter. Place on a greased baking sheet and bake for 10 to 12 minutes.

Unbaked dough will keep well in the refrigerator for up to two weeks.

nature rolls

yields 2½ to 3 dozen

1	cup shortening	2	(¼-ounce) packages active dry yeast
1	cup all bran cereal	1	cup warm water (105° to 115°)
¾	cup sugar	2	large eggs, lightly beaten
1½	teaspoons salt	6½	cups all-purpose flour
1	cup boiling water		

Combine shortening, cereal, sugar, salt and boiling water in a large bowl. Cool to luke-warm temperature.

Combine yeast and warm water in a small bowl; let stand 5 minutes. Stir yeast mixture and eggs into shortening mixture.

Add half of flour, beating well. Stir in remaining flour. Place in a greased bowl. Cover and refrigerate until ready to bake.

Shape dough into balls and place in greased muffin pans (dough should fill cups half full). Let rise 2 hours.

Preheat oven to 425°. Bake for 10 to 12 minutes.

pumpkin crescents

yields 3 dozen

1	(¼-ounce) package active dry yeast	⅓	cup sugar
1	cup warm water (105° to 115°)	1½	teaspoons salt
1	large egg, lightly beaten	5-6	cups all-purpose flour
1	cup canned pumpkin		butter, softened
½	cup shortening		

Combine yeast and water in a small bowl; let stand 5 minutes.

Combine egg, pumpkin, shortening, sugar and salt in a large bowl; stir in yeast mixture. Add 3 cups flour, beating until smooth. Stir in enough remaining flour to make a smooth dough.

Turn dough out on a floured surface. Knead for 5 minutes or until smooth and elastic. Place in a greased bowl, turning to coat top. Cover and let rise in a warm place until doubled in bulk.

Punch dough down and divide into three equal portions. Roll each portion into a 12-inch circle on a floured surface. Spread evenly with butter and cut into 12 wedges. Roll up each wedge beginning with rounded edge and place roll, with points tucked under, on a greased baking sheet. Cover slightly and let rise 30 to 45 minutes or until doubled in bulk.

Preheat oven to 400°. Bake for 15 to 20 minutes.

broccoli cornbread

yields 12 to 18 servings

1	(10-ounce) package frozen chopped broccoli, thawed	½	cup minced onion
4	large eggs, lightly beaten	¾	cup butter or margarine, melted
1	(12-ounce) container cottage cheese	2	(8.5-ounce) boxes cornbread mix
			vegetable cooking spray

Preheat oven to 350°. Cook broccoli according to package directions for 6 minutes; set aside.

Combine eggs, cottage cheese, onion and butter in a large bowl. Stir in cornbread mix and broccoli.

Spoon batter into a 13 x 9-inch baking pan coated with cooking spray. Bake for 30 to 35 minutes.

This moist and delicious bread is so rich that you don't need to butter it after baking.

cilantro batter bread

yields one loaf

1	tablespoon poppy seeds	1	cup 2% milk
4½	cups all-purpose flour, divided	2	tablespoons butter
1	(¼-ounce) package active dry yeast	1	(4-ounce) can chopped green chiles, drained
2	tablespoons sugar	½	cup fresh cilantro, chopped
1	teaspoon salt	3	tablespoons freeze dried chives
1	teaspoon garlic powder		
1	cup water		

Generously grease a 12-cup Bundt pan or 10-inch tube pan. Sprinkle bottom and sides with poppy seeds; set aside.

Combine 2 cups flour, yeast, sugar, salt and garlic powder in a large mixing bowl, stirring until well blended.

Combine water, milk and butter in a saucepan over medium-high heat. Heat until very warm (120° to 130°). Add to flour mixture, beating at medium speed with an electric mixer. Stir in remaining 2½ cups flour, chiles, cilantro and chives with a wooden spoon. Cover and let rise in a warm place for 45 to 60 minutes or until doubled in bulk.

Punch dough down and spoon into prepared pan. Cover loosely with greased plastic wrap and cloth towel. Let rise in a warm place for 30 to 45 minutes or until doubled in bulk.

Preheat oven to 375°. Uncover dough and bake for 35 to 40 minutes or until deep golden brown. Cool 5 minutes; remove from pan.

★ *poquito mas* ★

Cilantro-the dark green, lacy leaves of the coriander plant. Also called Chinese parsley and Mexican parsley, this herb has a bright, lively flavor and pungent fragrance. Cilantro is widely used in Mexican, South American, Asian and Caribbean cooking as its flavor complements spicy foods. Cilantro is generally sold in bunches and can be found year-round. Leaves should have a bright, even color with no sign of wilting. Store cilantro in a plastic bag in the refrigerator for up to 1 week. You can also place the bunch, stems down, in a cup of water. Cover with a plastic bag and change the water every 2 to 3 days. Wash and pat dry the leaves before using.

focaccia bread with assorted toppings

yields 6 to 8 servings

2	cups warm water (105° to 115°)	1	teaspoon salt
4	teaspoons active dry yeast	½	cup olive oil
	pinch sugar		cornmeal
4-5	cups bread flour, divided		topping

Combine water and yeast in a small bowl; sprinkle with sugar. Let stand 5 minutes (mixture should be foamy).

Combine 3 cups flour and salt in a large mixing bowl, blending well. Add yeast mixture and olive oil; beat for 3 minutes with a heavy-duty electric mixer. Stir in remaining 1 to 2 cups flour, ½-cup at a time. Turn dough out onto a floured surface; knead until elastic and forms a ball. Place dough in an oiled bowl. Cover and let rise in a warm place for 1½ hours.

Place dough on a lightly floured surface and press until flattened. Sprinkle cornmeal on a 15 x 10-inch jelly-roll pan and place dough in pan. Let rise 30 minutes.

Preheat oven to 450°. Poke holes at 1-inch intervals with fingers or the handle of a wooden spoon. Arrange topping on dough and bake for 30 minutes. Reduce oven temperature to 400° and bake until golden brown.

rosemary topping

⅓	cup olive oil	2	tablespoons fresh oregano, chopped
3	tablespoons fresh rosemary, chopped		

Combine oil, rosemary and oregano; brush evenly on dough.

focaccia bread *continued*

caramelized onion and brie

¼	cup butter		¼	cup sliced almonds
3	onions, sliced		8	ounces Brie cheese, rind removed
1	tablespoon balsamic or cider vinegar			

Melt butter in a large skillet over low heat. Add onions and cook, uncovered and stirring occasionally, for 30 minutes or until onions are very tender. Stir in vinegar; cook 10 minutes.

Spoon onions evenly over top of dough; sprinkle with almonds. Cut cheese into pieces and arrange evenly over the top.

calamata olives and thyme

1	tablespoon olive oil		1	tablespoon fresh thyme, minced
1	cup calamata olives, pitted and coarsely chopped			

Brush oil over dough. Sprinkle olive and thyme, pressing gently into dough.

roasted garlic and rosemary

6	large cloves garlic, halved lengthwise		1	tablespoon fresh rosemary, coarsely chopped
½	cup olive oil			coarse salt
				freshly ground black pepper

Preheat oven to 300° and place baking rack in lower third of oven. Combine garlic and oil in a small baking dish. Bake for 1 hour; cool on a wire rack for 30 minutes. Drizzle oil over dough and sprinkle evenly with rosemary, salt and pepper.

★ *poquito mas* ★

Focaccia is traditionally drizzled liberally with olive oil. The dough is seasoned with toppings of your choice. The assorted flavors of the toppings hit your palate with the first bite. Focaccia is often dipped in flavored olive oils when served.

pesto bread

yields 2 loaves

1½ (¼-ounce) packages active dry
    yeast
2   cups warm water (105° to 115°)
1   tablespoon sugar

1½ teaspoons salt
5-6 cups all-purpose flour
    pesto
    cornmeal

Combine yeast and water in a large bowl; stir in sugar and salt. Let stand 5 minutes (mixture should be foamy).

Add flour, one cup at a time, beating until forming a smooth dough. Turn dough out onto a floured surface and knead until smooth and elastic. Place dough in an oiled bowl and cover with a towel. Let rise in a warm place for 1½ hours or until doubled in bulk.

Punch down dough; turn out onto a floured surface and knead. Divide in half; press each half into a 12 x 10-inch rectangle. Spread pesto evenly on each rectangle and roll up, pinching ends to seal. Let rise 5 to 10 minutes.

Brush loaves with cold water. Sprinkle baking sheet with cornmeal and place loaves, seam side down, on cornmeal. Brush loaves with cold water and place in a cold oven. Heat oven to 400° and bake 35 to 40 minutes until golden brown and loaves sound hollow when tapped.

pesto

2   cups fresh basil leaves
½   cup fresh parsley
½   cup olive oil

1   teaspoon salt
2   cloves garlic
½   cup grated Parmesan cheese

Combine basil, parsley, oil, salt and garlic in the container of a blender or food processor. Process until very finely chopped. Pulse in cheese. Cover and store any remaining pesto in the freezer.

Salads and Soups

dreamy apricot salad

yields 12 to 15 servings

2	(3-ounce) packages apricot-flavored gelatin	1	(20-ounce) can crushed pineapple, undrained
⅔	cup sugar	1	(14-ounce) can sweetened condensed milk, chilled
⅔	cup water	1	(8-ounce) package cream cheese, softened
2	(4¾-ounce) jars pureed apricot baby food	1½	cups chopped nuts

Combine gelatin, sugar and water in a small saucepan over medium-high heat. Bring mixture to a boil, stirring to dissolve sugar and gelatin; remove from heat. Stir in pureed apricot and pineapple; let cool.

Combine condensed milk and cream cheese in a small bowl, beating until smooth. Stir into cooled gelatin mixture. Fold in nuts. Pour into a 9-cup mold. Cover and refrigerate until firm.

Carefully loosen gel from the side of container with a sharp knife. Dip container in warm water for 5 seconds. Invert plate over container; hold firmly and turn over. Lift container from gelatin.

mango jellied salad

yields 16 servings

3	(3-ounce) packages lemon-flavored gelatin	2	(8-ounce) packages cream cheese, softened and divided
3	cups boiling water	1	(26-ounce) jar mangoes, undrained and divided
3	tablespoons fresh lemon juice, divided		

Combine gelatin and boiling water; stir 2 minutes or until gelatin dissolves. Stir in 1½ tablespoons lemon juice; cool.

Combine 1 package cream cheese, half of mango and liquid and remaining 1½ tablespoons lemon juice in a blender; process until smooth. Stir into gelatin mixture.

Combine remaining cream cheese and mango in a blender; process until smooth. Stir into gelatin mixture. Pour into individual molds or a 13 x 9-inch baking dish. Cover and refrigerate until firm.

Serve on lettuce leaves with mayonnaise or a dressing of sour cream mixed with powdered sugar.

snapp salad

yields 12 to 15 servings

s   2 pints fresh strawberries, hulled

n   8 nectarines, pitted and cut into pieces

a   3 avocados, peeled, pitted and cut into pieces

p   3 pears, cored and cut into pieces

p   1 (15.25-ounce) can pineapple chunks, drained

apple cider dressing

Combine strawberry, nectarine, avocado, pear and pineapple in a serving bowl.

Pour dressing over fruit and serve.

apple cider dressing

yields approximately 2 cups

1   cup vegetable oil

¾   cup sugar

⅓   cup apple cider vinegar

1   tablespoon grated onion

1   teaspoon dry mustard

½   teaspoon salt

Combine oil, sugar, vinegar, onion, mustard and salt in a large jar; cover and shake vigorously.

spinach apple salad

yields 4 servings

| ½ | cup chopped walnuts | 2 | red delicious apples, cored and sliced dressing |
| 1 | (10-ounce) bag fresh spinach, trimmed | 1 | (4-ounce) package crumbled blue cheese |

Preheat oven to 350°. Place walnuts in a shallow pan. Bake for 5 minutes, stirring occasionally, or until toasted; cool.

Combine spinach, apples and walnuts in a large serving bowl; add dressing, tossing to coat. Sprinkle with blue cheese.

dijon dressing

yields approximately ⅔ cup

| ⅓ | cup olive oil | 1 | tablespoon Dijon mustard |
| ¼ | cup white wine vinegar | 1 | teaspoon sugar |

Combine oil, vinegar, mustard and sugar in a jar; cover and shake vigorously.

spinach and mandarin orange salad with caramelized almonds

yields 8 servings

1	head red or green leaf lettuce, shredded	1	(11-ounce) can Mandarin orange segments, drained
½	cup chopped celery		caramelized almonds or toasted nuts
⅓	cup chopped green onion		tarragon dressing

Combine lettuce, celery, onion, oranges and almonds in a large serving bowl; cover and refrigerate until chilled.

Toss salad with just enough dressing to coat.

caramelized almonds

yields ½ cup

2	tablespoons sugar	½	cup sliced almonds

Combine sugar and almonds in a small saucepan over low heat, shaking pan gently until sugar dissolves and almonds are coated. Pour onto greased foil; cool. Break into small pieces.

tarragon dressing

yields approximately ¾ cup

½	cup olive oil		dash hot pepper sauce
¼	cup tarragon vinegar	½	teaspoon salt
2	tablespoons sugar	¼	teaspoon black pepper
½	teaspoon Worcestershire sauce		

Combine oil, vinegar, sugar, Worcestershire sauce, hot pepper sauce, salt and pepper in a large jar. Cover and shake vigorously; refrigerate until ready to serve.

strawberry-spinach salad

yields 8 servings

1	(10-ounce) bag fresh spinach, trimmed		poppy seed dressing
1	pint strawberries, halved or 2 (11-ounce) cans Mandarin orange segments, drained		slivered almonds

Combine spinach and strawberries in a serving bowl. Add dressing, tossing to coat. Sprinkle with almonds.

poppy seed dressing

yields approximately 1½ cups

½	cup sugar		¼	teaspoon Worcestershire sauce
2	tablespoons sesame seeds		½	cup olive oil
1	tablespoon poppy seeds		¼	cup apple cider vinegar
1½	teaspoons minced onion		2	tablespoons water
¼	teaspoon paprika			

Combine sugar, sesame seeds, poppy seeds, onion, paprika and Worcestershire sauce in a blender.

Combine oil, vinegar and water. Turn blender on high; gradually add oil mixture in a slow, steady stream.

spinach and new potato salad

yields 6 to 8 servings

10	new potatoes (1¼ pounds)	1	cup chopped walnuts
1	tablespoon salt, divided	2	teaspoons chopped garlic
½	pound sliced bacon, cut into 1-inch pieces	½	cup olive oil
2	cups yellow onion, chopped	¼	cup balsamic vinegar
1	teaspoon freshly ground black pepper, divided	1	(10-ounce) bag fresh spinach, trimmed
		½	cup crumbled feta or blue cheese

Cook potatoes in a large saucepan with 1 teaspoon salt and boiling water to cover until tender. Quarter and set aside in a large bowl.

Cook bacon in a large skillet over medium-high heat for 10 minutes or until slightly crisp. Add onion, 1 teaspoon salt and ¼ teaspoon pepper. Sauté until onions are golden brown. Add walnuts and cook 5 minutes, stirring often; remove from heat. Add garlic and stir for 30 seconds. Add oil and vinegar, stirring until well blended.

Add ½ cup of the dressing and ½ teaspoon salt to potatoes, tossing until well coated. Transfer to another bowl; set aside.

Combine spinach, remaining 1½ cups dressing, remaining ½ teaspoon salt and remaining ¾ teaspoon pepper in the bowl, tossing until coated. Divide mixture on salad plates and top evenly with potatoes. Sprinkle with cheese and serve immediately.

laura welch bush

First Lady of Texas Laura Bush focuses on issues that are important to Texas families. Mrs. Bush's primary focus is education. Education has been an important part of her life, from childhood, throughout her career in public education and during her years as First Lady of Texas. She earned a bachelor of science degree in education from Southern Methodist University and a master of library science degree from the University of Texas at Austin.

Mrs. Bush has ten years of experience as an elementary school teacher and librarian. She is the founder and honorary chairman of the Texas Book Festival, an annual celebration of Texas books and authors that raises money for public libraries. In 1999, Mrs. Bush launched a statewide early childhood initiative, which helps parents and caregivers prepare young children for reading and learning before they enter school.

Governor and Mrs. Bush have been married since 1977. They are the proud parents of twin daughters, Barbara and Jenna, who were born in 1981 and are named after their grand-mothers.

The First Lady of Texas, Laura Bush has graciously contributed one of her favorite recipes, Southwestern Potato Salad, to the Junior League of Victoria.

laura bush's
southwestern potato salad

yields 6 to 8 servings

12	medium red potatoes, peeled if desired	½	cup mayonnaise or more to taste	
2	large hard-cooked eggs, diced	2	teaspoons whole-grain mustard	
¼	cup calamata olives, pitted and chopped	1	teaspoon chopped fresh cilantro	
2	pickled jalapeños, chopped	1	teaspoon chopped fresh oregano	
			salt	
			black pepper	

Cook potatoes in boiling water to cover 15 to 20 minutes or until tender. Rinse under cold running water. Slice or dice; place in a large mixing bowl.

Add eggs, olives and jalapeño, tossing gently until combined.

Combine mayonnaise, mustard, cilantro and oregano; stir gently into potato mixture. Season to taste with salt and pepper.

texas coleslaw

yields 8 servings

1	large cabbage, shredded	1	cup white wine vinegar
1	large onion, thinly sliced	1	tablespoon celery seeds
1	cup sugar	1	tablespoon dry mustard
2/3	cup vegetable oil		

Combine cabbage, onion and sugar in a large bowl, stirring until well blended.

Combine oil, vinegar, celery seeds and mustard in a saucepan over medium-high heat. Bring mixture to a boil, stirring constantly. Pour hot oil mixture over cabbage mixture, tossing well. Cover and refrigerate at least 8 hours.

tomato-pasta salad

yields 6 to 8 servings

16	ounces penne pasta, uncooked	8	ounces mozzarella cheese, cubed
5	large tomatoes, diced	1/3	cup olive oil
3	cloves garlic, minced	1	tablespoon crushed red pepper flakes
1	(4½-ounce) can chopped ripe olives	1	teaspoon minced fresh mint
½	cup chopped fresh basil		fresh basil sprig
½	teaspoon salt		
½	teaspoon pepper		

Cook pasta according to package directions; drain and rinse with cold water. Cool.

Combine tomato, garlic, olives, basil, salt and pepper in a large bowl. Top with pasta and cheese.

Combine oil, pepper flakes and mint in a small glass bowl. Microwave on HIGH for 60 seconds. Pour oil mixture over salad, tossing gently to combine. Cover and refrigerate until well chilled.

chinese cabbage salad

yields 8 to 10 servings

1	large napa or Chinese cabbage, thinly sliced	½	cup chopped green onion
		½	cup sliced or chopped radishes

Combine cabbage, green onion, radish, dressing and topping in a large serving bowl, tossing until well blended.

dressing

½	cup sugar	¼	cup vinegar
½	cup vegetable oil	1	tablespoon soy sauce

Combine sugar, oil, vinegar and soy sauce in a large jar; cover and shake vigorously. Refrigerate until ready to serve.

topping

¼	cup butter, melted	2	(3-ounce) packages ramen soup noodles, crushed
½	cup sliced almonds		
½	cup sunflower seeds		

Preheat oven to 350°. Combine butter, almonds, sunflower seeds and ramen noodles in a small bowl, stirring until coated. Place on a baking sheet and bake until golden brown; cool. Store in an airtight container until ready to serve.

Discard seasoning packet from ramen noodles or save for another use.

broccoli salad

Yields 6 servings

1	bunch broccoli, cut into florets		1	(8-ounce) can sliced water chestnuts, drained
10	slices crisp cooked bacon, crumbled		⅔	cup raisins
5	green onions, sliced			dressing

Blanch broccoli, if desired, in boiling water to cover for 1 to 3 minutes or until bright green. Immediately plunge in ice water to stop the cooking process; drain.

Combine broccoli, bacon, onion, water chestnuts and raisins in a large bowl. Add dressing, tossing to coat.

dressing

1	cup mayonnaise		2	tablespoons apple cider vinegar
¼	cup sugar			

Combine mayonnaise, sugar and vinegar in a small bowl. Cover and refrigerate until ready to use.

cucumber salad

yields 6 servings

2	large cucumbers, sliced	½	large sweet onion, thinly sliced

Combine cucumbers and onion in a bowl. Pour dressing over cucumber and onions, stirring until well blended. Cover and refrigerate several hours, stirring occasionally.

dressing

1	(5-ounce) can evaporated milk (not fat-free)	¼	cup white vinegar
⅓	cup sugar		salt
			black pepper

Combine milk, sugar, vinegar, salt and pepper in a large jar; cover and shake vigorously.

This salad will keep well in the refrigerator for 2 to 3 days.

fried okra salad

yields 8 servings

1 (12-ounce) package breaded okra
2 tomatoes, chopped
1 bunch green onions, sliced

6 slices crisp cooked bacon, crumbled
½ bell pepper, chopped
dressing

Fry okra according to package directions; drain.

Combine tomatoes, green onion, bacon, bell pepper and okra in a serving bowl.

Pour dressing over salad, tossing to coat. Serve warm.

dressing

¼ cup sugar
¼ cup oil

2 tablespoons vinegar

Combine sugar, oil and vinegar in a jar; cover and shake vigorously.

marinated vegetable salad

yields 8 servings

1	(15-ounce) can cut green beans, drained		1	(4-ounce) jar sliced mushrooms, drained
1	(15-ounce) can English peas, drained		1	(4-ounce) jar chopped pimientos, drained
1	(15.25-ounce) can whole kernel corn, drained		1	bunch green onions, chopped
1	(8-ounce) can sliced water chestnuts, drained		¾	cup chopped bell pepper
			⅔	cup chopped celery
				dressing

Combine beans, peas, corn, water chestnuts, mushroom, pimiento, onion, bell pepper and celery in a 13 x 9-inch baking dish. Pour dressing over vegetables. Cover and refrigerate 24 hours before serving.

dressing

¾	cup sugar		1	teaspoon salt
¾	cup vinegar		1	teaspoon black pepper
½	cup oil			

Combine sugar, vinegar, oil, salt and pepper in a saucepan. Bring mixture to a boil, stirring until sugar dissolves; cool.

pepperoni pasta salad

yields 6 to 8 servings

1	(9-ounce) package spinach fettuccine, cut into thirds	1-2	(3.5-ounce) packages sliced pepperoni, halved
1	bunch broccoli florets	6	green onions, thinly sliced
1	zucchini, thinly sliced	1	red bell pepper, cut into strips
1	(10-ounce) package frozen whole kernel corn	1	green bell pepper, cut into strips
1	(10-ounce) package frozen English peas	1	stalk celery, thinly sliced
		1	(8-ounce) bottle zesty Italian salad dressing
			grated Parmesan or Romano cheese

Cook pasta according to package directions; drain and rinse with cold water. Blanch broccoli in boiling water to cover for 1 to 3 minutes or until bright green. Remove with a slotted spoon and immediately plunge in ice water to stop the cooking process and drain on paper towels. Repeat with zucchini, corn and peas.

Combine pasta, broccoli, zucchini, corn, peas, pepperoni, onion, bell pepper and celery in a large bowl. Add dressing, tossing to coat. Sprinkle with cheese. Cover and refrigerate until ready to serve.

chicken salad with south of the border cranberry sauce

yields 2 to 3 cups

3	large bone-in chicken breasts	½	cup sliced almonds
	celery leaves		mayonnaise
1½	cups thinly sliced celery		south of the border cranberry sauce

Combine chicken breasts, celery leaves and water to cover in a large saucepan over medium-high heat. Bring to a boil; reduce heat and simmer 1½ hours or until tender. Cut breasts into chunks, discarding skin and bones.

Combine chicken, celery and almonds in a bowl. Add enough mayonnaise to desired consistency, stirring until well blended. Cover and refrigerate 2 hours before serving. Serve with cranberry sauce.

south of the border cranberry sauce

1	(16-ounce) can whole berry cranberry sauce	1	tablespoon finely chopped fresh cilantro
1	(10.5-ounce) jar hot jalapeño pepper jelly (red)		

Combine cranberry sauce, jelly and cilantro in a saucepan over low heat. Cook, stirring often, until jelly melts; cool. Cover and refrigerate until ready to use.

pollo picado

yields 6 cups

1	(3½-pound) roasted or boiled whole chicken	2	tablespoons chopped fresh cilantro
2	tomatoes, chopped	2	tablespoons chopped fresh oregano
2-4	jalapeños, chopped	2	avocados, cubed and tossed with lime juice
2	green onions, chopped	2-4	tablespoons fresh lime juice
½	red onion, chopped		shredded lettuce
⅓	pound Monterey Jack cheese, cut into ½-inch cubes		fresh oregano sprigs
½	teaspoon whole white peppercorns		chopped tomato
½	teaspoon whole comino seeds (cumin)		red onion rings
¼	teaspoon whole coriander seeds		cheese cubes
	salt		lime wedges
			salsa picante
			chile rajas

Shred chicken, discarding skin and bones. Combine chicken, tomato, jalapeño, onion and cheese in a large bowl.

Combine peppercorns, comino seeds and coriander seeds in a small skillet over medium heat. Cook until lightly toasted; cool. Place toasted mixture in a spice grinder; process until finely ground.

Add ground spices, salt, cilantro and oregano to chicken mixture, stirring until well blended. Just before serving, add avocado and lime juice, tossing well.

Serve mounded on a platter of shredded lettuce with fresh oregano. Garnish with chopped tomato, red onion rings, cheese cubes, lime wedges, salsa picante and chile rajas.

This recipe can easily be doubled or tripled.

chicken artichoke salad

yields 10 servings

1   (6.9-ounce) package chicken-
     flavored rice and pasta mix

1   (14-ounce) can artichoke hearts,
     drained and chopped

1   (4-ounce) can sliced mushrooms,
     drained

1   (4.25-ounce) can chopped ripe olives

1   bunch green onions (green part
     only), chopped

1   green bell pepper, chopped

⅓   cup oil

⅓   cup vinegar

⅓   cup mayonnaise

2   tablespoons lemon juice

¼   teaspoon seasoned salt

     salt

     black pepper

     lemon pepper

4   chicken breasts, cooked and cubed

Cook rice mix according to package directions; cool.

Combine artichoke heart, mushroom, olive, onion and bell pepper in a large bowl. Combine oil, vinegar, mayonnaise, lemon juice and seasoned salt. Stir into artichoke mixture, blending well. Season to taste with salt, black pepper and lemon pepper.

Stir in chicken and rice. Cover and refrigerate 2 hours or overnight.

chicken and pesto salad

yields 8 servings

6-10 **boneless chicken breasts**
      zesty Italian salad dressing, divided
1-2   **red bell peppers**
½   **pound snow peas**
1-2   **(9-ounce) packages refrigerated angel hair pasta**

1-2   **(.75-ounce) packages pesto sauce mix**
      olive oil
½-1   **pound fresh spinach, trimmed**
1   **(2.25-ounce) can sliced ripe olives, drained**
      toasted almonds

Combine chicken breast and most of dressing in a large resealable plastic bag or shallow container. Cover and refrigerate 8 hours or overnight, turning occasionally. Preheat grill. Grill chicken breasts 5 to 7 minutes on each side or until tender, but not dry. Place cooked breasts in a shallow container and top with remaining dressing. Cover and set aside. When cool enough to handle, slice chicken into strips; set aside.

Preheat oven to broil with rack 5 to 7 inches away from heat. Cut peppers into quarters and remove stems, ribs and seeds. Place on a foil-lined baking sheet. Broil peppers for 10 to 15 minutes until skin is blistered and charred. Transfer to plastic bags to steam for 15 minutes; peel skin and discard. When cool enough to handle, slice peppers into strips.

Blanch snow peas in boiling water to cover for 1 to 3 minutes or until bright green. Immediately plunge in ice water to stop the cooking process. Set aside.

Cook pasta according to package directions; drain and rinse with cold water.

Prepare sauce according to package directions using olive oil and water. Combine pasta and sauce in a large bowl. Stir in chicken, roasted pepper, peas, spinach and olives. Sprinkle with almonds.

mandarin chicken salad

yields 6 servings

3   cups diced cooked chicken
1   cup diced celery
2   tablespoons lemon juice
1   tablespoon minced onion
½   teaspoon salt
1   cup seedless grapes
⅓   cup mayonnaise

1   (2-ounce) package slivered almonds, toasted
1   (11-ounce) can Mandarin orange segments, drained
leaf lettuce
orange slices
grape clusters

Combine chicken, celery, lemon juice, onion and salt in a large bowl. Cover and refrigerate until well chilled.

Add grapes, mayonnaise and almonds, stirring until well blended. Fold in orange segments. Serve salad on lettuce and garnish with orange slices and grape clusters, if desired.

mexican shrimp salad

yields 6 servings

1 pound cooked shrimp, peeled and deveined

⅓ cup sliced green onions

⅓ cup olive oil

⅓ cup liquid from pickled jalapeño slices

2 tomatoes, chopped

1 (7-ounce) jar stuffed green olives, drained and chopped

2 tablespoons minced fresh parsley or cilantro

½ teaspoon minced fresh oregano

salt

black pepper

1 large avocado, pitted and sliced

¼ cup pickled jalapeño slices

Combine shrimp, green onion, oil and liquid in a large bowl, mixing well. Cover and refrigerate for 2 hours.

Stir in tomato, olives and parsley. Season to taste with salt and pepper. Cover and refrigerate 2 hours. Add avocado and jalapeño just before serving.

For a pretty presentation, serve in a margarita or martini glass.

this can't be tuna salad

yields 12 servings

1 (6-ounce) package long grain and wild rice

2 (6-ounce) cans spring water tuna, drained

1 cup salted cashews, coarsely chopped

1 cup mayonnaise

½ cup sour cream

2 tablespoons dried green bell pepper

1 tablespoon dried chopped onion

1 tablespoon Crazy Jane's Mixed Up Salt or seasoned salt

½ teaspoon crushed red pepper flakes

Prepare rice according to package directions; cool.

Combine rice, tuna, cashews, mayonnaise, sour cream, bell pepper, onion, salt and pepper flakes. Cover and refrigerate at least 4 hours before serving. Serve on a bed of mixed lettuce, croissants, hollowed out sourdough roll or in an avocado half.

This recipe is best prepared at least one day in advance so the nuts can soften and all of the flavors can blend. It also freezes well.

tex-mex soup

yields 6 to 8 servings

2	pounds lean ground beef
1	onion, chopped
2	cloves garlic, minced
1	(15-ounce) can black beans, undrained
1	(15-ounce) can kidney beans, undrained
1	(15-ounce) can pinto beans, undrained
1	(14.5-ounce) can diced tomatoes, undrained
1	(15-ounce) can whole kernel corn, undrained
1	(10-ounce) can diced tomatoes with chiles
1	(1-ounce) package buttermilk salad dressing mix
1	(1.25-ounce) package taco seasoning mix
2	cups water
	salt
	black pepper

Combine beef, onion and garlic in a large soup pot over medium-high heat. Cook, stirring constantly, until beef is brown; drain.

Stir in beans, tomatoes, corn, tomatoes with chiles, dressing mix, seasoning mix and water, adding more water, if desired. Cook over medium heat until desired consistency and thoroughly heated. Season to taste with salt and pepper. Serve as is or top with tortilla strips, shredded cheese, sour cream, avocado, and chopped cilantro.

Freezes well.

wonderful chili

yields 6 to 8 servings

1	tablespoon vegetable oil	2	(14½-ounce) cans stewed tomatoes
2	cloves garlic, minced	1	(8-ounce) can tomato sauce
2	onions, finely chopped	1	(6-ounce) can tomato paste
1	green bell pepper, finely chopped	1	(4-ounce) can diced green chiles
1	stalk celery, finely chopped	¼	cup chili powder
2	pounds lean ground beef	¼	cup chili sauce
2	pounds ground turkey	1	jalapeño, chopped
2	cups water	1	teaspoon salt

Heat oil in a large soup pot or Dutch oven over medium-high heat. Add garlic, onion, bell pepper, and celery; sauté until tender. Add beef and turkey; cook, stirring constantly, until meat is brown.

Add water, tomatoes, tomato sauce, tomato paste, green chiles, chili powder, chili sauce, jalapeño and salt, stirring until well blended. Bring mixture to a boil; reduce heat and simmer 1 hour. Adjust seasonings, if necessary.

Serve with green salad and cornbread twists or toasted cornbread. Delicious!

southwest white chili

yields 4 to 6 servings

2	tablespoons olive oil	2	teaspoons ground cumin
2	pounds boneless chicken breasts, cut into pieces	2	teaspoons dried oregano
½	cup chopped onion	2	teaspoons chopped fresh cilantro
2	cups chicken broth	½	teaspoon cayenne pepper
1	(8-ounce) can chopped green chiles	2	(15-ounce) cans white cannellini or navy beans, undrained
2	teaspoons garlic powder		shredded Monterey Jack cheese
			sliced green onions

Heat oil in a 4-quart saucepan over medium-high heat. Add chicken; sauté 4 to 5 minutes, stirring often. Remove chicken with a slotted spoon; cover and keep warm.

Add onion and sauté for 2 minutes. Stir in broth, chiles, garlic powder, cumin, oregano, cilantro and cayenne. Bring mixture to a boil; reduce heat and simmer for 30 minutes.

Stir in reserved chicken and beans; simmer for 10 minutes. Garnish each serving with cheese and onions.

vegetarian chili

yields 8 to 10 servings

2	tablespoons vegetable oil		1	tablespoon ground cumin
1	cup chopped green or red bell pepper		2	(14½-ounce) cans vegetable or chicken broth
1	cup chopped onion		2	(15-ounce) cans black beans rinsed and drained
2	tomatoes, peeled and chopped or 1 (14½-ounce) can stewed tomatoes		2	(10-ounce) packages frozen whole kernel corn, thawed
3	jalapeños, seeded and chopped		1	(15-ounce) can pinto beans, rinsed and drained
2	zucchini, diced		¼	cup fresh cilantro, chopped
2	yellow squash, diced			
2	tablespoons chili powder			

Heat oil in a large soup pot or Dutch oven over medium heat. Add bell pepper and onion; sauté until tender. Stir in tomatoes. Cook, stirring occasionally, for 5 minutes. Stir in jalapeño, zucchini, yellow squash, chili powder and cumin; cook 1 minute.

Stir in broth, black beans, corn and pinto beans. Bring mixture to a boil; reduce heat, and simmer for 20 minutes. Garnish each serving with fresh cilantro.

creamy tomato-basil soup

yields 6 to 8 servings

4	cups canned whole tomatoes	½	cup unsalted butter, softened
4	cups unsalted tomato juice	¼	teaspoon cracked black pepper
12-14	fresh basil leaves		salt
1	cup heavy whipping cream		

Combine tomatoes and juice in a saucepan. Bring mixture to a boil; reduce heat to medium-low, and simmer for 30 minutes. Cool slightly. Transfer mixture in batches to the container of blender or food processor; add basil and process until pureed.

Return mixture to saucepan; stir in cream and butter. Cook over low heat, stirring constantly, until mixture is well blended. Stir in pepper. Season to taste with salt.

This freezes well. If you can't find unsalted tomato juice, use regular tomato juice and omit salt.

Rockin' the Flavors of Texas

cream of jalapeño soup

yields 8 servings

5	tablespoons butter or margarine, divided	1	large green bell pepper, finely chopped
3	tablespoons all-purpose flour	5	jalapeños, seeded and finely diced
3	cups chicken broth	1	cup (4 ounces) shredded Swiss cheese
2	cups heavy whipping cream	1	cup (4 ounces) shredded cheddar cheese
1	large onion, minced		salt
1	large carrot, peeled and finely diced		

Melt 3 tablespoons butter in a large, heavy saucepan over low heat. Add flour, whisking until smooth. Cook 1 minute, whisking constantly. Gradually add broth and cream; cook over medium heat for approximately 10 minutes, whisking constantly, until mixture is thickened and bubbly. Set aside.

Melt remaining 2 tablespoons butter in a small skillet over low heat. Add onion, carrot and bell pepper. Sauté for 8 minutes, stirring constantly, or until tender. Stir in jalapeños.

Add cheeses to cream mixture, stirring until cheese melts. Add vegetable mixture, stirring until well blended. Season to taste with salt.

For spicier soup, add more jalapeños.

★ poquito mas ★

Jalapeño chile- these hot to very hot chiles are named after Jalapa, the capital of Veracruz, Mexico. Jalapeños have rounded tips and are about 2 inches long and about 1 inch in diameter. They turn from dark green to scarlet red when ripe. Jalapeños are widely available and are used both fresh and canned in a variety of dishes. Dried jalapeños are called chipotles.

cream of red pepper soup

yields 6 servings

4-5	large red bell peppers		dash ground nutmeg
2	tablespoons unsalted butter		dash cayenne pepper
½	cup finely chopped onion		salt
½	cup minced shallots		black pepper
1	tablespoon all-purpose flour	1	cup heavy whipping cream
3	cups chicken broth	2-4	sprigs fresh cilantro, minced

Preheat oven to broil with oven rack placed 3 to 5 inches from heat. Cut peppers into quarters and remove stems, ribs and seeds. Place on a foil-lined baking sheet. Broil peppers 3 inches from heat for 10 to 15 minutes until skin is blistered and charred. Transfer to plastic bags to steam for 15 minutes; peel skin and discard.

Melt butter in a large saucepan over medium heat. Add onion and shallots; sauté for 3 minutes or until transparent. Add flour; cook 1 minute, stirring constantly. Gradually stir in broth. Bring mixture to a boil; reduce heat and simmer, covered, for 20 minutes. Add roasted pepper; simmer for 5 minutes. Stir in nutmeg and cayenne. Season to taste with salt and pepper.

Transfer mixture to a blender; process until smooth. Return soup to saucepan over low heat; cook until thoroughly heated. Stir in cream. Garnish each serving with cilantro.

This soup can be served hot or cold. Milk may be substituted to decrease fat content. Pureed mixture (without cream) freezes well. You can roast the red bell peppers and freeze until a later use.

sherried brie soup

yields 4 servings

2	cups cream sherry		4	ounces Brie cheese, rind removed
2	tablespoons butter		2	cups heavy whipping cream
1½	pounds sliced fresh mushrooms		1	teaspoon salt
⅔	cup minced shallots		½	teaspoon black pepper
2	teaspoons fresh lemon juice			minced fresh chives
2	tablespoons all-purpose flour			chopped Brie
4	cups beef stock			

Cook sherry in a medium saucepan over medium-high heat until reduced by half; set aside.

Melt butter in a medium skillet over medium-high heat. Stir in mushrooms, shallots and lemon juice. Sauté for 2 minutes. Add flour, stirring until well blended. Cook 1 minute, stirring constantly.

Gradually add stock and reduced sherry. Bring mixture to a boil; reduce heat and simmer for 25 minutes. Add Brie, stirring until cheese melts. Stir in cream, salt and pepper. Garnish each serving with chives and Brie.

★ poquito mas ★

Shallot- similar in shape to garlic, shallots are composed of numerous cloves, covered in a thin, papery skin. The skin can vary in color from tan to gray or rose, and the white flesh is often tinged with green or purple. Shallots have a more delicate flavor than an onion, but may be used in the same manner. Choose dry-skinned shallots that are firm and plump with no sign of wrinkling or sprouting. Store dry shallots in a cool, dry, well-ventilated place for up to a month. Fresh shallots can be refrigerated for up to a week.

cream of portobella mushroom soup

yields 6 to 8 servings

3	tablespoons unsalted butter
1	pound portobella mushrooms, quartered and thinly sliced
1	onion, chopped
4½	cups water

1½	cups heavy whipping cream
6	tablespoons medium-dry sherry
	salt
	black pepper
6	tablespoons thinly sliced fresh chives

Melt butter in a large, heavy saucepan over medium heat. Add mushroom and onion; sauté until tender and liquid evaporates. Stir in water and cream. Bring mixture to a boil; reduce heat and simmer for 15 minutes.

Place half of soup in a blender; process until smooth. (You may also use an immersion blender and process directly in the soup pot.) Stir pureed mixture into soup. Add sherry and season to taste with salt and pepper. Cook soup over medium heat until thoroughly heated; stir in chives.

zesty pumpkin soup

yields 6 to 8 servings

¼	cup butter or margarine
1	cup chopped onion
1	clove garlic, crushed
1	teaspoon curry powder
½	teaspoon salt
⅛-¼	teaspoon ground coriander
⅛	teaspoon crushed red pepper flakes, optional
3	cups chicken broth
1	(15-ounce) can pumpkin
1	cup half-and-half
	sour cream
	chives

Melt butter in a large saucepan over medium-high heat. Add onion and garlic; sauté until tender. Stir in curry, salt, coriander and pepper flakes; cook 1 minute.

Stir in broth. Bring mixture to a boil; reduce heat and simmer, uncovered, for 15 to 20 minutes. Stir in pumpkin and half-and-half. Cook 5 minutes.

Transfer in batches to a blender; process until smooth. Serve warm and garnish with a dollop of sour cream and chopped chives, if desired.

carrot-ginger soup

yields 6 servings

6	tablespoons butter	3	carrots, peeled and cut into ½-inch pieces
1	large onion, chopped	2	tablespoons lemon juice or to taste
¼	cup peeled and finely chopped fresh ginger		curry powder
3	cloves garlic, chopped		salt
7	cups chicken broth		black pepper
1	cup dry white wine		

Melt butter in a large soup pot over medium heat. Add onion, ginger and garlic; sauté 15 minutes. Add broth, wine and carrot. Bring mixture to a boil; reduce heat and simmer for 45 minutes.

Transfer soup in batches to a blender or food processor; process until smooth. Season to taste with lemon juice, curry, salt and pepper.

fossati's broccoli-cheese soup

yields 20 servings

2 (10-ounce) packages frozen chopped broccoli, thawed
2 quarts chicken broth
1 cup butter or margarine
1¼ cups all-purpose flour
1 teaspoon salt
1 teaspoon ground cumin
½ teaspoon white pepper
3 pints half-and-half
processed cheese sauce

Combine broccoli and broth in a large soup pot. Bring to a boil; reduce heat and simmer until broccoli is tender.

Melt margarine in a large saucepan over medium heat; add flour, whisking until smooth. Cook 1 minute, whisking constantly. Stir in salt, cumin and pepper. Gradually add half-and-half; cook over medium heat, whisking constantly, until mixture is thickened and bubbly.

Stir cream sauce into chicken broth mixture, stirring until well blended. Stir in cheese sauce to taste.

★ poquito mas ★

This recipe is served at Fossati's Deli, the oldest delicatessen in Texas, and is a favorite among customers.

potato-bacon soup

yields 6 servings

2	small onions, minced		2	tablespoons butter
¾	cup Canadian bacon, chopped		¼	teaspoon salt
4	medium potatoes (1½ pounds), peeled and cubed		⅛	teaspoon black pepper
2	cups water			shredded cheddar cheese
1	(12-ounce) can evaporated milk			low fat sour cream
				chives or finely sliced green onions

Combine onion and bacon in a large saucepan over medium heat; sauté until tender. Stir in potato and water. Bring mixture to a boil; reduce heat and simmer for 10 to 15 minutes. Slightly mash potatoes.

Stir in milk, butter, salt and pepper. Cook over medium heat, stirring constantly until slightly thickened and thoroughly heated. (Do not boil.) Garnish each serving with cheese, sour cream and chives.

For a thicker soup, combine 2 teaspoons cornstarch and ½ cup water. Stir in with milk.

potato and cabbage soup

yields 8 servings

¼	cup butter or margarine		½	teaspoon dried basil
1	head cabbage, chopped			salt
1	onion, chopped			black pepper
3	potatoes, peeled and diced		1	(10¾-ounce) can nacho cheese soup
4	cups water		1	cup (4 ounces) shredded cheddar cheese
2	tablespoons chicken bouillon granules		2	cups milk
½	teaspoon dried thyme			

Melt butter in a large soup pot over medium-high heat. Add cabbage and onion. Sauté until tender. Add potato, water, bouillon, thyme, basil, salt and pepper. Bring mixture to a boil; reduce heat and simmer for 20 to 25 minutes or until potatoes are soft.

Stir in soup, cheese and milk. Cook, stirring constantly, until cheese melts and soup is thoroughly heated.

tortilla soup

yields 6 to 8 servings

2	ancho chiles		1	tablespoon fresh thyme
2	pasilla or anaheim chiles			reserved chicken from chicken stock
	vegetable oil for frying		1	bunch fresh spinach, optional
8-10	corn tortillas, sliced into thin strips			salt
1	tablespoon vegetable oil			black pepper
1	onion, chopped		2	avocados, chopped
2-3	cloves garlic, minced		2	tablespoons fresh lime juice
	chicken stock			fresh spinach leaves
2-3	(14.5-ounce) cans chicken broth		1	cup fresh cilantro leaves
2	sliced zucchini, optional			shredded cheese
1	tablespoon fresh oregano			lime wedges

Prepare chicken stock recipe; set aside shredded chicken.

Remove stems and seeds from dried chiles. Lightly toast on an ungreased griddle for 30 seconds (do not burn or the peppers will turn bitter). Set aside.

Heat oil in a skillet over medium-high heat. Add tortilla strips and fry until golden brown; drain on paper towels and set aside.

Heat oil in a large saucepan over medium-high heat. Add onion and garlic; sauté until translucent. Stir into chicken stock.

Add reserved chiles, canned chicken broth and zucchini, if desired. Bring mixture to a boil; reduce heat and simmer for 25 minutes. Stir in oregano, thyme, reserved chicken and spinach, if desired; simmer for 15 minutes. Season to taste with salt and pepper.

Combine avocados and lime juice in a small bowl; set aside. Place a few leaves of fresh spinach in individual bowls. Add cilantro and cheese. Ladle soup into serving bowls and garnish with avacado and lime wedges.

tortilla soup *continued*

chicken stock

1	(3½-4-pound) chicken, cut into pieces	2	bay leaves
2	carrots, cut into pieces	1	teaspoon ground cumin
2	stalks celery, cut into pieces		peppercorns
1	onion, quartered	8-10	cups water

Place chicken, carrot, celery, onion, bay leaves, cumin and peppercorns in a large soup pot. Add water. Bring mixture to a boil, skimming residue from top. Reduce heat, and simmer over low heat, uncovered, until chicken is tender.

Remove chicken from broth. Pull meat from chicken into shreds, discarding skin and bones; set aside. Strain broth, discarding vegetables, and return to soup pot.

chicken pasta soup

yields 10 to 12 servings

4½	quarts (9 cups) chicken broth	2	cloves garlic, minced
7	ounces cheese tortellini	1	cup cooked rice
1	pound boneless chicken, cut into ½-inch pieces		salt
1	(10-ounce) bag fresh spinach		black pepper
1	small red bell pepper, diced		grated Parmesan cheese

Bring broth to a boil in a large saucepan over medium-high heat. Add tortellini and cook for 4 to 6 minutes. Stir in chicken, spinach, bell pepper, garlic and rice. Cook for 5 minutes or until chicken is tender. Season to taste with salt and pepper. Sprinkle each serving with cheese.

tortellini soup

yields 4 to 6 servings

1	tablespoon olive oil	¼	teaspoon black pepper
1	onion, chopped	1	(9-ounce) package refrigerated tortellini
2	cups chopped zucchini		
1	teaspoon minced garlic	2	cups frozen whole kernel corn, optional
2	(14.5-ounce) cans chicken broth		
2	tomatoes, chopped	4-5	tablespoons grated Parmesan or Romano cheese
⅓	cup fresh basil, chopped		

Heat oil in a large saucepan over medium heat. Add onion, zucchini and garlic; sauté until tender. Stir in broth, tomato, basil and pepper. Bring mixture to a boil; reduce heat and simmer for 10 minutes.

Stir in tortellini and corn, if desired. Simmer for 5 to 6 minutes or until tortellini are tender. Sprinkle each serving with cheese.

cold zucchini soup

yields 8 servings

5	cups chicken broth		2	(8-ounce) packages cream cheese, cubed and softened
4	zucchini, quartered and sliced		1	tablespoon chopped fresh dill
1	bunch green onions, chopped		1	(8-ounce) container sour cream
1	teaspoon salt			chopped fresh chives
1	teaspoon black pepper			

Combine broth, zucchini, green onion, salt and pepper in a large saucepan. Bring to a boil; reduce heat and simmer, stirring occasionally, for 20 minutes. Add cream cheese and dill, stirring until well blended.

Transfer in batches to a blender; process until smooth. Cover and refrigerate 8 hours; stir in sour cream. Garnish each serving with fresh chives, if desired.

To lighten, use fat-free chicken broth, reduced-fat sour cream and reduced-fat cream cheese. This soup may also be served warm.

rio dulce gazpacho

yields 16 to 20 servings

20	peeled tomatoes or 2 (28-ounce) cans whole tomatoes, undrained
1	onion, quartered
1	unpeeled cucumber, coarsely chopped
1	green bell pepper, cut into pieces
1	small head of garlic, peeled
½	cup chopped parsley
4	cups chicken stock
1	(46-ounce) can tomato juice
¾	cup olive oil
½	cup vinegar
	salt
	black pepper
	hot sauce
2	rolls or French bread slices, torn into pieces

Combine tomato, onion, cucumber, bell pepper and garlic in a blender or food processor (in batches, if necessary); process until finely chopped.

Combine chopped vegetables, parsley, stock, tomato juice, olive oil and vinegar in a large bowl, stirring until well blended.

Season to taste with salt, pepper and hot sauce. Add rolls, stirring until well blended and soup is slightly thickened. Cover and refrigerate until chilled. Serve cold.

This gazpacho comes from a marina on the Rio Dulce in Guatemala. If tomatoes are not in season, use canned. This recipe makes over a gallon so you will need a very large container or bowl.

Side Dishes

artichoke sauté

yields 6 to 8 servings

½	head garlic		salt
	boiling water		pepper
2	tablespoons olive oil		thyme or mixed dried herbs
1	(9-ounce) package frozen artichoke hearts, thawed and drained	2	tablespoons butter
2	large onions, halved and sliced	1	tablespoon white or red wine vinegar
1½	tablespoons fresh lemon juice		minced fresh parsley

Separate garlic cloves from head and drop in boiling water for 1 minute to loosen skins. Remove skins and slice in half lengthwise or cut into quarters.

Heat oil in a large skillet over medium-high heat. Add garlic, artichoke hearts, onion and lemon juice; sauté until onions are tender. Season to taste with salt, pepper and herbs.

Add butter; cover and simmer for 10 minutes, stirring occasionally, or until artichokes are tender. Add vinegar; cover and cook 5 minutes. Adjust seasonings and sprinkle with parsley.

To serve cold: chill artichoke mixture. Before serving, toss with additional lemon juice, olive oil and fresh minced parsley.

marinated asparagus

yields 6 servings

2-3	pounds asparagus, trimmed	¼	cup olive oil
1	bunch green onions, chopped	3	tablespoons sweet pickle relish
1	(2-ounce) jar chopped pimientos, drained	1	tablespoon dried parsley
¾	cup vegetable oil		salt
⅓	cup tarragon vinegar		pepper

Cook asparagus in boiling, salted water for 6 minutes. Drain and immediately immerse in ice water to stop the cooking process.

Combine onion, pimiento, vegetable oil, vinegar, olive oil, relish and parsley in the container of a blender or food processor. Process until well blended. Season to taste with salt and pepper.

Drain asparagus and arrange in an oblong dish. Pour marinade over asparagus. Cover and refrigerate at least 2 hours. Serve asparagus over lettuce leaves, drizzling marinade on top, if desired.

Recipe can be covered and stored in the refrigerator for up to one week.

broccoli soufflé

yields 6 servings

1   (10-ounce) package frozen
    chopped broccoli, thawed
1   (10¾-ounce) can cream of
    mushroom soup

1   cup mayonnaise
3   large eggs, beaten
1   tablespoon grated onion
    pepper

Preheat oven to 325°. Cook broccoli according to package directions; drain. Combine broccoli, soup, mayonnaise, eggs, onion and pepper in a large bowl, stirring until well blended. Pour into a greased 1-quart baking dish.

Bake for 45 minutes or until set in the center.

This recipe can be mixed in the morning and baked for dinner. Easily doubled.

sicilian broccoli

yields 4 to 6 servings

1   bunch broccoli, cut into florets
¼   cup butter
2   cloves garlic, minced

½   cup sliced ripe olives
    freshly grated Parmesan cheese

Arrange broccoli in a steamer basket over boiling water. Cover and steam until crisp-tender. Place in a serving dish; keep warm.

Melt butter in a small saucepan over medium heat. Add garlic and sauté until tender. Stir in olives; cook until thoroughly hot. Pour over broccoli and sprinkle with cheese.

spicy black beans with rice

yields 4 to 6 servings

3	tablespoons olive oil		3	tablespoons red wine vinegar
1	large red bell pepper, chopped		½	teaspoon ground cumin
1	onion, minced			salt
2	serrano chiles, finely chopped			pepper
3	cloves garlic, minced			hot cooked white or brown rice
2	(15-ounce) cans black beans, undrained			salsa

Heat oil in a large skillet over medium-high heat. Add bell pepper, onion, chile and garlic. Sauté until tender. Stir in beans, vinegar and cumin.

Bring mixture to a boil; reduce heat and simmer 5 minutes. Season to taste with salt and pepper. Serve over rice and top with salsa.

salsa

2	tomatoes, diced		1	large clove garlic, minced
1	bunch green onions, chopped		½	bunch fresh cilantro, chopped
1	serrano chile, finely chopped		2-3	tablespoons fresh lime juice

Combine tomato, onion, chile, garlic, cilantro and juice in a serving bowl. Cover and refrigerate before serving to allow flavors to blend.

★ poquito mas ★

History of beans and rice- these foods traveled well, which is why they are featured in so many Texas dishes. Chuck wagon cooks filled their wagon drawers and cowboys would pack their saddlebags with dried beans and rice to cook on the trail. Because beans were served so often, cowboys began to call mealtime "bean time".

carrot soufflé

yields 8 to 10 servings

1	pound carrots, peeled and sliced	3	tablespoons all-purpose flour
½	cup butter or margarine, melted	1	teaspoon baking powder
3	large eggs	1	teaspoon vanilla extract
1	cup sugar		

Preheat oven to 350°. Cook carrot in boiling, salted water to cover until tender; drain.

Combine carrot and butter in a blender; process until smooth. (You may also mash carrots in a mixing bowl with an electric mixer.) Add eggs, sugar, flour, baking powder and vanilla. Process until well blended. Spoon mixture into a greased 1½-quart baking dish. Bake for 45 minutes or until firm.

corn and bacon casserole

yields 6 servings

6	slices bacon	½	teaspoon pepper
½	cup chopped onion	1	cup sour cream
2	tablespoons all-purpose flour	4	cups frozen whole kernel corn, thawed
2	cloves garlic, minced	1	tablespoon chopped fresh parsley
½	teaspoon salt	1	tablespoon chopped fresh chives

Preheat oven to 350°. Cook bacon in a large skillet over medium-high heat until crisp. Drain, reserving 2 tablespoons drippings. Crumble bacon and set aside.

Heat drippings over medium heat; add onion and sauté until tender. Stir in flour, garlic, salt and pepper; cook 1 minute stirring constantly.

Remove from heat and stir in sour cream. Add corn, parsley and half of reserved bacon, stirring until well blended. Pour mixture into a greased 1-quart baking dish. Sprinkle with remaining bacon. Bake for 20 to 25 minutes or until thoroughly heated. Sprinkle with chives.

green bean bundles

yields 6 servings

1	**cup butter**
1	**cup firmly packed light brown sugar**
½	**cup apple cider vinegar**
1	**teaspoon soy sauce**

½	**teaspoon garlic salt**
2	**(14½-ounce) cans uncut green beans, drained or 1½ pounds fresh blanched green beans**
	bacon slices, halved

Melt butter in a small saucepan over medium heat. Add sugar, vinegar, soy sauce and garlic salt, stirring until well blended. Remove from heat.

Arrange a bundle of green beans (approximately 10 beans) and wrap with bacon. Place in a 13 x 9-inch baking dish. Repeat with remaining beans and bacon. Pour butter mixture over beans; cover and refrigerate 8 hours or overnight.

Preheat oven to 350°. Bake, uncovered for 30 minutes.

The beans do not have to be marinated overnight, but the taste is enhanced if you do.

green bean mushroom bake

yields 8 to 10 servings

3	(10-ounce) packages frozen French style green beans, thawed and drained	3	cups half-and-half
½	cup butter	1	teaspoon salt
1	(8-ounce) package mushrooms, sliced	1	teaspoon Ac'cent
1	onion, chopped	½	teaspoon black pepper
¼	cup all-purpose flour	2	teaspoons soy sauce
		¼	teaspoon hot sauce
		¾	cup (3 ounces) shredded cheddar cheese

Preheat oven to 325°. Cook beans according to package directions; drain and set aside.

Melt butter in a large saucepan over medium-high heat. Add mushroom and onion; sauté until tender. Stir in flour. Cook 1 minute, whisking constantly.

Gradually add half-and-half; stirring until well blended. Stir in salt, Ac'cent, black pepper, soy sauce, hot sauce and cheese. Cook over medium heat, whisking constantly, until mixture is thickened and bubbly.

Combine sauce and green beans; pour into a greased 13 x 9-inch baking dish. Bake for 30 minutes.

gruyère cheese grits

yields 6 to 8 servings

4	cups milk	½	teaspoon white pepper
1	cup grits	⅓	cup butter, melted
½	cup butter	1	cup (4 ounces) shredded Gruyère cheese
1	large egg, lightly beaten		
1	teaspoon salt	½	cup freshly grated Parmesan cheese

Preheat oven to 350°. Bring milk to a boil in a large saucepan over medium heat, stirring frequently. Add grits and butter, stirring until butter melts. Cook for 5 minutes, stirring constantly, or until the consistency of oatmeal. Remove from heat.

Stir a small amount of the hot grits mixture into the egg. Add egg mixture back into grits mixture, stirring until well blended. Stir in salt, white pepper, melted butter and Gruyère, blending well.

Spoon into a greased 2-quart baking dish. Sprinkle with Parmesan cheese. Bake for 1 hour, covering with foil, if necessary, to prevent overbrowning.

This dish is very rich and easy to prepare.

baked 1015 onion soufflé

yields 8 servings

2	tablespoons butter or margarine	2	cups (8 ounces) shredded mozzarella cheese
1	pound Texas 1015 or other sweet onion, sliced	2	tablespoons all-purpose flour
1	(10¾-ounce) can cream of chicken soup	2	large eggs, lightly beaten

Preheat oven to 350°. Melt butter in a medium skillet over medium heat. Add onion and sauté 5 minutes until translucent.

Combine onions, soup, cheese, flour and eggs, stirring until well blended. Pour into a greased 8 x 8-inch baking dish.

Bake for 25 to 30 minutes or until golden brown and bubbly. Serve with sliced French bread or crackers.

★ *poquito mas* ★

Tearless Texans- Texas 1015 SuperSweet and Texas SpringSweet are the first fresh onions you will find in the market each spring. Harvested from March until June, the sweet onions are grown in South Texas' fertile Rio Grande Valley. The mild taste of Texas sweet onions is due to their high water content. They are composed of 35 percent water, as compared to the 10% water volume of regular storage onions. Texas 1015 SuperSweet Onions are usually planted on the fifteenth day of the tenth month, hence the 1015 moniker.

onion pudding

yields 8 to 10 servings

½	cup butter	2	teaspoons salt
6	cups thinly sliced sweet onion	6	large eggs
3	tablespoons all-purpose flour	2	cups heavy whipping cream
2	tablespoons sugar	3	egg whites
2	teaspoons baking powder		

Melt butter in a large skillet over medium heat. Add onion and cook 30 to 45 minutes or until golden brown; cool.

Preheat oven to 350°. Coat a 3-quart baking dish with olive oil; set aside.

Combine flour, sugar, baking powder and salt; set aside.

Beat eggs in a large mixing bowl at medium-high speed with an electric mixer. Stir in whipping cream. Gradually beat in flour mixture, a small amount at a time, until well blended. Add onion to cream mixture, stirring well.

Beat egg whites in a mixing bowl at high speed with an electric mixer until stiff peaks form. Fold into onion mixture. Pour into prepared baking dish and bake for 45 minutes or until set.

Excellent served with a rib roast or roasted turkey.

state fair pinto beans

yields 18 to 24 servings

1	pound pinto beans	2	(28-ounce) cans tomatoes
	fat back, cut into strips	2	cups firmly packed light brown sugar
½	cup butter	2	tablespoons white vinegar
2	onions, chopped		salt
2	green bell peppers, chopped		black pepper
2	tart apples, chopped		grated Parmesan cheese
2	teaspoons curry powder or to taste		

Place beans and fat back in a large soup pot or Dutch oven; add water 2 inches above beans. Soak beans 8 hours; drain.

Place beans in pot with water to cover; bring to a boil Cover, reduce heat, and simmer 1½ hours or until beans are tender.

Preheat oven to 350°. Melt butter in a skillet over medium-high heat. Add onion, bell pepper, apple and curry powder; sauté until tender.

Place tomatoes in a colander, pressing down until all liquid is removed. Combine tomatoes, onion mixture, beans, brown sugar, vinegar, salt and pepper in a large bowl, stirring until well blended. Pour into a lightly greased baking dish.

Bake for 30 minutes. Sprinkle with Parmesan cheese before serving.

scalloped jalapeño potatoes

yields 8 to 10 servings

4	pounds baking potatoes	2	cups milk
	salt	1	(6-ounce) package refrigerated garlic-flavored process cheese
	black pepper		
1	cup butter, melted and divided	1	(6-ounce) package refrigerated jalapeño-flavored process cheese
8	green onions, chopped		
1	green bell pepper, chopped	1	(4-ounce) jar pimientos, drained
2	tablespoons all-purpose flour		

Cook potatoes in boiling water to cover until tender; cool. Peel, sliced and arrange in the bottom of a lightly greased baking dish. Season to taste with salt and pepper; set aside.

Preheat oven to 350°. Melt ½ cup butter in a large skillet over medium-high heat. Add onion and bell pepper; sauté until tender.

Combine flour and remaining ½ cup butter in a large bowl, stirring until well blended. Stir in milk, garlic cheese, jalapeño cheese, pimiento and onion mixture. Pour mixture over potatoes and bake 45 minutes, uncovered, until hot and bubbly.

twice baked jalapeño potatoes

yields 8 servings

4	large baking potatoes	½	cup warm milk
	vegetable oil	½	cup sour cream
⅓	cup butter, melted and divided	1	tablespoon minced fresh chives or green onion
1	onion, coarsely chopped		
1	cup (4 ounces) shredded sharp cheddar cheese, divided	1	teaspoon salt
		¼	teaspoon black pepper
1	cup (4 ounces) shredded mozzarella cheese, divided	1	large egg
		8	slices crisp-cooked bacon, crumbled
4-5	pickled jalapeños, minced with seeds		

Preheat oven to 400°. Lightly coat potatoes with oil and bake for 1 hour or until tender. Set aside to slightly cool. Reduce oven temperature to 325°.

Heat 1½ tablespoons butter in a skillet over medium-high heat. Add onion and sauté until tender; set aside.

Cut potatoes in half lengthwise and carefully scoop flesh into a mixing bowl, leaving a ¼-inch shell. Place potato shells on a baking sheet.

Add remaining ¼ cup butter, ⅔ cup cheddar cheese, ⅔ cup mozzarella cheese, jalapeño, milk, sour cream, chives, salt, pepper and egg to potato flesh, stirring until well blended. Spoon mixture evenly into potato shells. Sprinkle with remaining cheese and bacon. Bake for 20 minutes or until thoroughly heated.

chunky two-cheese potatoes with garlic and pesto

yields 12 servings

5	large baking potatoes, cut into ½-inch pieces		2	tablespoons minced shallots
2	cups heavy whipping cream		2	tablespoons prepared pesto
6	sun-dried tomatoes, packed in oil, drained and minced		¼	teaspoon white pepper
2	tablespoons minced garlic		1½	cups (6 ounces) shredded mozzarella cheese
			1½	cups (6 ounces) shredded Jarlsberg cheese

Preheat oven to 375°. Place potatoes in an 18 x 12-inch rimmed baking sheet. Combine cream, tomato, garlic, shallot, pesto and white pepper in a bowl, stirring until well blended. Pour over potatoes, stirring gently to coat. Sprinkle evenly with cheese.

Bake for 45 minutes or until potatoes are tender and cheese is golden brown. Cool 10 minutes before serving.

whipped potatoes

yields 6 to 8 servings

2½	pounds baking potatoes, peeled and quartered	¼	cup butter, softened
1	(3-ounce) package cream cheese, softened	½	teaspoon garlic salt
¾	cup sour cream		salt
			black pepper
			paprika

Preheat oven to 350°. Cook potato in boiling, salted water to cover for 15 minutes or until tender; drain. Mash potatoes in a large bowl. Add cream cheese, sour cream, butter, garlic salt, salt and pepper, stirring until well blended.

Spoon mixture into a greased 1½-quart baking dish. Sprinkle with paprika. Bake, uncovered, for 30 minutes or until thoroughly heated.

This recipe may be served just after mixing ingredients. Spoon warm potato mixture into a serving bowl and sprinkle with paprika.

potato and herb bake

yields 6 to 8 servings

½	teaspoon salt	6	tablespoons butter or margarine, melted
¼	teaspoon dried basil	2	pounds baking potatoes, peeled and thinly sliced
¼	teaspoon dried thyme	6	tablespoons finely chopped onion
¼	teaspoon black pepper		

Preheat oven to 425°. Combine salt, basil, thyme and pepper in a small bowl; set aside. Coat bottom of a 13 x 9-inch baking dish with 2 tablespoons butter. Layer one-third potatoes, seasoning mixture, onion and butter. Repeat layers twice.

Press layers down and cover tightly with foil. Bake for 20 minutes. Uncover and bake 20 minutes or until potatoes are tender. Remove from oven and let stand 10 minutes before serving.

rice pilaf with basil and pine nuts

yields 3 to 4 servings

1	(14½-ounce) can chicken or beef broth	⅓	cup chopped fresh basil or 1½ teaspoons dried
1½	tablespoons olive oil	¼	cup pine nuts, toasted
½	large onion, chopped		salt
1	cup uncooked long grain rice		black pepper

Bring broth to a boil in a small saucepan; reduce heat to low and keep warm.

Heat oil in a heavy saucepan over medium heat. Add onion and sauté for 6 minutes or until translucent. Add rice and cook, stirring constantly, for 1 minute.

Stir in broth and bring mixture to a boil. Cover; reduce heat and simmer for 20 minutes or until broth is absorbed and rice is tender. Stir in basil and nuts. Season to taste with salt and pepper. Serve immediately.

This recipe may be doubled or tripled.

spanish rice with green chiles

yields 4 servings

1	tablespoon olive oil
1	cup uncooked long grain rice
2-3	cups beef broth
1	(8-ounce) can tomato sauce

1	(4-ounce) can diced green chiles, drained
1	teaspoon ground cumin
½	teaspoon seasoned salt
¼	cup sliced onion, optional

Heat oil in a saucepan over medium-high heat. Add rice and sauté until light brown. Stir in broth and tomato sauce. Bring mixture to a boil; reduce heat to low. Stir in chiles, cumin and salt. Cover and simmer until all liquid is absorbed and rice is tender, adding more broth, if necessary. Add sliced onion, if desired, and cook until onion is tender.

This recipe can be easily doubled or tripled as needed to serve a crowd.

spinach puff

yields 4 servings

1	(10-ounce) package frozen chopped spinach, thawed		2	tablespoons butter, melted
1	tablespoon finely chopped green onion		1	cup grated Parmesan cheese
3	large eggs, lightly beaten		1	tablespoon all-purpose flour
½	cup sour cream		¼	teaspoon salt
			⅛	teaspoon ground nutmeg
				dash black pepper

Preheat oven to 350°. Cook spinach according to package directions, adding onion to pan as the spinach cooks; drain very well.

Combine eggs, sour cream, butter, cheese, flour, salt, nutmeg and pepper in a large bowl. Add spinach mixture, stirring until well blended. Spoon into a greased 1-quart baking or soufflé dish. Bake for 25 to 30 minutes or until center is set.

This recipe can be easily halved or doubled. Adjust baking time accordingly.

sweet potato casserole

yields 12 servings

2 (15-ounce) cans sweet potatoes, drained and mashed
2 cups sugar
4 large eggs
1 cup milk

⅔ cup butter or margarine, melted
1 teaspoon salt
2 teaspoons vanilla extract
topping

Preheat oven to 350°. Combine sweet potatoes, sugar, eggs, milk, melted butter, salt and vanilla in a large mixing bowl, beating until smooth. Pour into a greased 13 x 9-inch baking dish.

Sprinkle topping evenly on sweet potato mixture. Bake for 1 hour or until center is firm.

topping

1 cup firmly packed light brown sugar
1 cup chopped pecans

½ cup all-purpose flour
⅓ cup butter, softened

Combine brown sugar, pecans, flour and butter in a small bowl, stirring until mixture is crumbly.

tomato-basil tart

yields 4 to 8 servings

1	(9-inch) pie crust		4	cloves garlic
1½	cups (6 ounces) shredded mozzarella cheese, divided		½	cup mayonnaise
5	plum tomatoes or 4 medium tomatoes		¼	cup grated Parmesan cheese
1	cup loosely packed fresh basil		⅛	teaspoon ground white pepper
				fresh basil leaves

Preheat oven to 375°. Bake pie shell according to package directions. Remove from oven and sprinkle bottom with ½ cup mozzarella cheese. Set aside and cool.

Cut tomato into wedges and drain on paper towels. Arrange tomato on cheese in pie shell.

Combine basil and garlic in a food processor; pulse until coarsely chopped, scraping down sides as necessary. Sprinkle over tomato.

Combine remaining 1 cup mozzarella cheese, mayonnaise, Parmesan cheese and pepper in a medium bowl. Spoon over basil mixture, spreading evenly to cover the top.

Bake for 35 to 40 minutes or until golden brown and bubbly. Serve warm and garnish with basil leaves, if desired.

tomato and zucchini gratin

yields 4 servings

1	pound Creole or beefsteak tomatoes, cut into ¼-inch slices	1	cup fine dry bread crumbs	
1	pound zucchini, cut into ¼-inch slices	½	cup finely chopped fresh, mild herbs (basil, chervil, tarragon, etc.)	
3	tablespoons olive oil, divided	½	cup grated Parmesan cheese	
	salt		fresh parsley	
	black pepper			

Preheat oven to 400°. Combine tomato and zucchini in a large bowl; drizzle with 1 tablespoon olive oil, tossing to coat. Sprinkle both sides of tomato and zucchini with salt and pepper; set aside.

Combine bread crumbs, herbs, cheese, remaining 2 tablespoons olive oil, salt and pepper.

Layer tomato and zucchini in four, lightly greased gratin dishes. Top evenly with bread crumb mixture.

Bake for 15 to 20 minutes or until golden brown. Garnish with parsley, if desired.

parmesan squash bake

yields 8 to 10 servings

12-15	yellow squash, sliced		½	cup slivered almonds, toasted
10	slices bacon		2	teaspoons salt
1	large onion, diced		½	teaspoon black pepper
10-12	green onions, sliced		3-4	cups fresh bread crumbs
1	cup half-and-half		2	cups grated Parmesan cheese

Preheat oven to 350°. Cook squash in boiling, salted water until tender. Drain and cut into small pieces.

Cook bacon in a large skillet over medium-high heat until crisp; remove bacon, reserving drippings in skillet. Crumble bacon and set aside.

Heat drippings over medium-high heat. Add onion and green onion; sauté until tender. Combine squash, bacon, onion, half-and-half, almonds, salt and pepper in a large bowl, stirring until blended. Spoon into a greased 13 x 9-inch baking dish or three small pie plates.

Combine bread crumbs and cheese; sprinkle over squash mixture. Bake for 20 minutes or until hot and bubbly.

sicilian tart

yields 12 servings

1	refrigerated pie crust
1½	cups (6 ounces) shredded mozzarella cheese, divided
¾	cup ricotta cheese
1	cup diced zucchini
½	cup drained and diced roasted red bell pepper
¼	cup chopped fresh basil or 1 tablespoon dried

Preheat oven to 375°. Place pie crust in 9-inch pie plate according to package directions. Combine 1¼ cups mozzarella cheese, ricotta, zucchini and peppers, stirring until well blended.

Spread mixture over crust, leaving a 1-inch border. Fold crust edges over filling and flute. Bake for 35 minutes or until golden brown.

Combine remaining ¼ cup mozzarella and basil; sprinkle over tart and let stand at least 10 minutes. Cut into 12 wedges and serve warm or at room temperature.

Cheese mixture may be prepared, covered and refrigerated up to 2 hours before assembling. Light cheese may be used. Delicious as an appetizer or a side dish.

sonora casserole

yields 6 to 8 servings

2	cups tomato sauce	3	cups sliced zucchini
1½	tablespoons chili powder	1	cup frozen corn kernels, thawed
1	tablespoon white wine vinegar	1	(4-ounce) can diced green chiles, drained
¼	teaspoon ground cumin	1½	cups (6 ounces) shredded cheddar cheese, divided
¼	teaspoon cayenne pepper		
¼	teaspoon garlic powder	¾	cup sour cream
	salt	2	green onions, thinly sliced
1	teaspoon vegetable oil		
6	corn tortillas, cut into strips		

Preheat oven to 350°. Combine tomato sauce, chili powder, vinegar, cumin, cayenne pepper, garlic and salt in a saucepan over medium heat. Simmer gently.

Heat oil in a skillet over medium-high heat. Add tortilla strips and fry until golden brown and crisp; drain on paper towels.

Arrange zucchini in a steamer basket over boiling water. Cover and steam until tender; drain.

Combine zucchini, tortilla strips, corn, chiles and ¾ cup cheese. Spoon into a greased 13 x 9-inch baking dish. Top with tomato sauce; sprinkle with remaining ¾ cup cheese. Bake, uncovered for 30 minutes until hot and bubbly. Remove from oven and spread sour cream on top. Sprinkle with green onions.

zucchini jack casserole

yields 6 servings

3 tablespoons all-purpose flour
2 teaspoons baking powder
½ teaspoon salt
4 large eggs, lightly beaten
½ cup milk
2 pounds small zucchini, sliced ¼-inch thick

3 cups (12 ounces) shredded Monterey Jack cheese
1 small onion, finely chopped
1 (7-ounce) can diced green chiles
¼ cup chopped fresh parsley
1 clove garlic, minced
1 cup seasoned croutons
3 tablespoons butter or margarine, melted

Preheat oven to 350°. Combine flour, baking powder, salt, eggs and milk, stirring until smooth. Stir in zucchini, cheese, onion, chiles, parsley and garlic. Spoon into a greased 13 x 9-inch baking dish.

Combine croutons and butter, stirring until coated. Sprinkle on casserole. Bake, uncovered, for 35 to 45 minutes.

zucchini pie

yields 8 servings

3 tablespoons butter
4 cups thinly sliced zucchini (approximately 4 medium)
1 cup chopped green onions
¼-½ cup chopped fresh parsley
2 cloves garlic, minced
¾ teaspoon dried basil
½ teaspoon salt
¼ teaspoon black pepper
2 large eggs, lightly beaten
1½ cups (6 ounces) shredded mozzarella cheese
2 teaspoons dry mustard
1 (11-ounce) package refrigerated breadstick dough or frozen pie crust, thawed

Preheat oven to 375°. Melt butter in a skillet over medium-high heat. Add zucchini, green onion, parsley, garlic, basil, salt and pepper; sauté until tender.

Combine eggs, cheese and mustard in a large bowl. Stir in zucchini mixture.

Line a 7- to 10-inch quiche pan or pie plate with breadstick dough (or use pie crust) and spoon in zucchini mixture. Bake for 20 to 25 minutes.

baked zucchini with mushrooms

yields 8 to 10 servings

3	zucchini, chopped		dash garlic salt
½	cup chopped mushrooms	½	cup butter, melted
¼	cup chopped onion	1	large egg, lightly beaten
3	slices crisp-cooked bacon, crumbled	1½	cups saltine cracker crumbs
½	teaspoon salt	½	cup (2 ounces) shredded Swiss or mozzarella cheese
¼	teaspoon black pepper		

Preheat oven to 350°. Combine zucchini, mushrooms, onion, bacon, salt, pepper, garlic salt, butter, egg and cracker crumbs in a large bowl, stirring until well blended.

Spoon into a greased 13 x 9-inch baking dish and top with cheese. Bake for 40 minutes or until hot and bubbly.

squash dressing

yields 8 to 10 servings

½	cup butter	1	(10¾-ounce) can cream of chicken soup
½	cup chopped onion	5	cups crumbled cornbread
½	cup chopped green bell pepper	3	cups cooked yellow squash
½	cup chopped celery	1	teaspoon salt
2	cups milk	½	teaspoon black pepper

Preheat oven to 325°. Melt butter in a skillet over medium-high heat. Add onion, bell pepper and celery; sauté until tender.

Combine milk and soup. Stir in onion mixture, cornbread, squash, salt and pepper. Spoon into a greased 13 x 9-inch baking dish and bake for 50 minutes.

cornbread dressing

yields 8 to 10 servings

1	(6-ounce) package yellow cornbread mix	7	pieces white bread, toasted and torn into pieces
2	tablespoons butter	20	saltine crackers, crushed
8	stalks celery, chopped	2-3	hard-cooked eggs, chopped
2	bunches green onions, chopped		dash curry powder
1	green bell pepper, chopped		salt
1	small white onion, chopped		black pepper
			chicken or turkey broth

Preheat oven to 350°. Prepare cornbread according to package directions; cool. Crumble cornbread in a large bowl and set aside.

Melt butter in a large skillet over medium-high heat. Add celery, green onion, bell pepper and onion; sauté until tender.

Combine cornbread, celery mixture, bread, crackers, eggs, curry, salt and pepper. Stir in enough chicken broth until mixture is very moist.

Spoon into a greased oblong baking dish. Bake for 45 minutes.

oyster dressing

yields 6 to 8 servings

turkey giblets
1 tablespoon olive oil
1 cup diced onion
1 cup diced celery
½ cup diced green bell pepper
½ loaf sliced white bread, toasted and torn into pieces
½ loaf sliced wheat bread, toasted and torn into pieces
2 cups chicken broth
1 pint fresh oysters, cut into pieces
2 eggs, lightly beaten

Preheat oven to 300°. Combine giblets and 2 cups of water in a saucepan over medium-high heat. Bring to a boil; reduce heat and simmer until done. Drain, chop and set aside.

Heat oil in a skillet over medium-high heat. Add onion, celery and bell pepper; sauté until tender.

Combine giblets, onion mixture, bread pieces and broth, stirring until well blended. Stir in oysters, adding more broth, if necessary (mixture should look soupy). Stir in eggs.

Spoon into a lightly greased 5-quart baking pan. Bake 1 hour, covered, or until firm.

summer vegetable casserole

yields 6 to 8 servings

8	cups lightly salted water		2	cloves garlic, minced
3	cups green beans, cut diagonally into 2-inch pieces		2	tablespoons all-purpose flour
2½	cups bow tie pasta		½	teaspoon salt
2	yellow squash, cut into thin strips		¼	teaspoon black pepper
2	tablespoons butter		2¼	cups skim milk
2	cups sliced mushrooms		½	cup shredded Swiss cheese
1	cup chopped onion		1-2	tablespoons Dijon mustard
3	tablespoons snipped fresh basil or 1½ teaspoons dried			hot sauce
2	tablespoons snipped fresh oregano or 1 teaspoon dried		4-6	plum tomatoes, diagonally sliced
			1	cup soft bread crumbs (approximately 1½ slices)
			¼	cup grated Parmesan cheese

Bring water to a boil in a 4-quart saucepan or Dutch oven. Add beans and cook, loosely covered, for 5 minutes. Add pasta. Return mixture to a boil; cook 5 minutes. Add squash. Return mixture to a boil; cook 5 minutes or until vegetables and pasta are tender. Drain and set aside.

Preheat oven to 400°. Melt butter in a large skillet over medium-high heat. Add mushroom, onion, basil, oregano and garlic; sauté until tender. Stir in flour, salt and pepper. Cook 1 minute, stirring constantly. Add milk; cook over medium heat, stirring constantly, until mixture is slightly thickened and bubbly. Stir in Swiss cheese, mustard and hot sauce; cook 1 minute.

Combine vegetable-pasta mixture and sauce in a large bowl. Add tomatoes, tossing until blended. Spoon mixture into a greased 3-quart or 13 x 9-inch baking dish. Combine bread crumbs and Parmesan cheese; sprinkle over casserole. Bake, uncovered, for 20 to 25 minutes or until thoroughly heated.

vegetable pie

yields 4 to 6 servings

1   tablespoon olive oil
1   large onion, sliced in rings
1   small eggplant, peeled and sliced
2   large tomatoes, peeled and sliced
½   teaspoon black pepper

1   (6-ounce) container pesto sauce or two cheese pesto
1   (9-inch) unbaked refrigerated pie crust

Preheat oven to 400°. Heat oil in a skillet over medium-high heat. Add onion and sauté until tender.

Layer half of onion, eggplant, tomato, pepper and pesto in a 9-inch pie plate. Repeat layers and top with pie crust. Place pie on a baking sheet and bake for 30 to 35 minutes.

two cheese pesto

2   cups fresh basil
6-8   sprigs fresh flat-leaf parsley
2-3   cloves garlic
½   cup pine nuts or walnuts
½   cup olive oil

⅓   cup grated Romano cheese
⅓   cup grated Parmesan cheese
   salt
   black pepper

Combine basil, parsley, garlic, nuts, oil, cheeses, salt and pepper in a food processor. Process until finely chopped.

Entrées

marinated stuffed beef tenderloin

yields 10 to 12 servings

1	tablespoon plus 1 teaspoon vegetable oil, divided	½	cup soy sauce	
1	pound fresh mushrooms, sliced	⅓	cup dry white wine	
1	bunch green onions, chopped	2	cloves garlic, minced	
¼	cup chopped fresh parsley	2	tablespoons light brown sugar	
1	(4-pound) beef tenderloin, trimmed	2	tablespoons honey	
		1	cup water	

Heat 1 teaspoon oil in a large skillet over medium heat. Add mushroom, onion and parsley. Sauté for 10 minutes or until all liquid evaporates; cool.

Make a 1-inch deep cut lengthwise along the top of the tenderloin; spoon mushroom mixture into opening. Tie tenderloin with cotton string at 1-inch intervals; place in a large shallow dish.

Combine soy sauce, wine, garlic, brown sugar, honey and remaining 1 tablespoon oil; pour over tenderloin. Cover and refrigerate 2 to 8 hours, turning occasionally.

Preheat oven to 425°. Remove tenderloin from marinade, reserving marinade. Place tenderloin on a lightly greased rack in a roasting pan. Pour water in roasting pan.

Bring reserved marinade to a boil in a small sauccpan; boil 1 minute. Bake tenderloin for 1 hour and 10 minutes or until a meat thermometer inserted in the thickest part registers 145° to 160°. Baste occasionally with marinade and cover with foil the last 30 minutes of cooking. Let stand 10 minutes before slicing.

filet mignon with lemon-peppercorn sauce

yields 4 servings

4	(8- to 10-ounce) center cut prime filet mignon steaks		pepper
	salt	¼	cup corn oil

Season filets with salt and pepper. Heat oil in a cast iron grill skillet over medium-high heat. Cook until desired degree of doneness. Serve hot with lemon-peppercorn sauce.

lemon-peppercorn sauce

2	tablespoons butter, divided	2	teaspoons crushed pink peppercorns
2	tablespoons minced white onion	1	teaspoon minced fresh thyme
1	clove garlic, minced	1	tablespoon all-purpose flour
1	cup beef broth	2-3	teaspoons freshly grated lemon peel
3	ounces (approximately ⅓ cup) red wine	¼	teaspoon kosher salt

Melt 1 tablespoon butter in a saucepan over medium-high heat. Add onion and sauté until tender. Add garlic; sauté 1 to 2 minutes. Stir in broth and wine. Bring mixture to a boil; reduce heat and simmer 5 minutes or until slightly reduced. Stir in peppercorns and thyme.

Combine remaining 1 tablespoon butter and flour into a paste. Add to sauce, whisking until well blended. Cook 3 to 4 minutes until smooth and slightly thickened. Stir in lemon peel and salt.

Green or black peppercorns may be substituted.

steak diane

yields 4 servings

2 tablespoons butter
2 cloves garlic, minced
2 cups sliced fresh mushrooms
4 (4-ounce) filet mignon steaks
2 tablespoons beef broth

1 tablespoon fresh lemon juice
1 tablespoon Dijon mustard
1 teaspoon Worcestershire sauce
2 tablespoons chopped green onion

Melt butter in a large, nonstick skillet over medium heat. Add garlic and mushrooms; sauté until tender. Remove from skillet and set aside.

Add steak to skillet; cook steak over medium heat 6 to 7 minutes per side, or until desired degree of doneness. Transfer to a serving platter; keep warm.

Add beef broth, lemon juice, mustard and Worcestershire to skillet. Bring mixture to a boil; reduce heat and simmer 2 minutes. Stir in reserved mushroom mixture; cook until thoroughly heated. Stir in green onions. Pour over steaks and serve immediately.

cajun rib-eye burgundy

yields 4 servings

4	(6-ounce) rib-eye steaks, cut 1-inch thick	1	tablespoon finely chopped fresh thyme
3	tablespoons Cajun seasoning	1	tablespoon finely chopped fresh rosemary
	salt	1	teaspoon minced garlic
	black pepper	1	cup Burgundy wine
1	tablespoon olive oil		
2	tablespoons chopped fresh oregano		

Rub steaks on both sides with seasoning, salt and pepper. Heat a heavy skillet over high heat. Cook steaks for 2 minutes on each side or until browned. Remove from skillet.

Reduce heat to medium and add oil. Add oregano, thyme, rosemary and garlic; sauté until fragrant and light brown. Stir in wine. Bring mixture to a boil; reduce heat to low and return steaks to skillet.

Cover and simmer for 10 minutes, turning once. Transfer steaks to a serving platter and keep warm.

Bring liquid to a boil; boil until reduced by half. Spoon sauce over steaks and serve.

salsa steak

yields 6 servings

¼	cup shortening	¼	cup sliced ripe olives, or more to taste
1½	cups sliced fresh mushrooms	2	teaspoons chili powder
½	cup chopped onion	1	teaspoon salt
¼	cup chopped green bell pepper	1¼-1½	pounds round steak, cut 1-inch thick
1	cup tomato sauce		

Preheat oven to 350°. Melt shortening in a large skillet over medium-high heat. Add mushrooms, onion and bell pepper; sauté for 5 minutes.

Stir in tomato sauce, olives, chili powder and salt.

Place steak in a greased 13 x 9-inch baking dish and pour sauce over meat. Cover and bake for 1½ hours or until tender.

beer and mustard marinated flank steak

yields 4 to 6 servings

1	(12-ounce) can beer, room temperature
¼	cup firmly packed light brown sugar
2	tablespoons dry mustard
2	tablespoons vegetable oil
1	tablespoon salt
2	teaspoons onion powder
1	teaspoon garlic powder
1	teaspoon black pepper
1½	pounds flank steak
	topping

Combine beer, sugar, mustard, oil, salt, onion powder, garlic powder and pepper in a large shallow dish. Add steak, turning to coat. Pierce steak on both sides with a fork. Cover and refrigerate at least 30 minutes up to 24 hours, turning occasionally.

Prepare barbecue grill. Remove steak from marinade, discarding marinade. Grill steak 4 to 5 minutes on each side or to desired degree of doneness.

Preheat oven to broil with oven rack 5 inches from heat. Place steak on a broiler pan and spread with topping. Sprinkle with cheese. Broil 2 minutes or until cheese melts. Slice at an angle (against the grain) to serve.

topping

1	tablespoon butter
1	onion, sliced
1	green bell pepper, sliced
1	(8-ounce) package mushrooms, halved
½	cup (2 ounces) shredded Swiss cheese

Melt butter in a large skillet over medium-high heat. Add onion, bell pepper and mushroom; sauté 4 to 5 minutes until tender.

The topping is optional. You can enjoy the steak right after grilling.

beer braised beef short ribs

yields 4 servings

5	pounds beef short ribs, trimmed	½	teaspoon dried thyme
3½	cups beef broth	¼	cup unsulfered molasses
1	(12-ounce) bottle dark beer	2	tablespoons balsamic vinegar
1	onion, sliced	2½	teaspoons hot pepper sauce
2	teaspoons salt, divided		

Preheat oven to 350°. Combine ribs, broth, beer, onion, 1 teaspoon salt and thyme in a large soup pot or Dutch oven over medium heat. Bring mixture to a boil. Cover and bake for 2 hours and 50 minutes or until ribs are very tender. Refrigerate until fat solidifies. (Recipe can be prepared to this point up to two days ahead.)

Spoon fat from surface of braising liquid. Remove ribs and pat dry. Strain braising liquid, reserving ¼ cup liquid. Combine reserved liquid, molasses, vinegar, hot sauce and remaining 1 teaspoon salt in a small bowl.

Prepare barbecue grill for medium heat. Grill ribs, covered, for 10 minutes or until crisp and hot, turning and basting frequently with molasses mixture.

slow bake brisket

yields 12 to 15 servings

1	(8-ounce) bottle Italian dressing		paprika
	garlic powder		onion powder
	coarse black pepper		white pepper
	Worcestershire sauce	2	sheets heavy-duty foil, twice as long as baking pan
	mesquite liquid smoke		
	cayenne pepper	1	(6 to 8-pound) whole brisket

Preheat oven to broil with baking rack in top position. Combine dressing, garlic powder, black pepper, Worcestershire sauce and liquid smoke in a small bowl. Stir in equal amounts of cayenne, paprika, onion powder and white pepper.

Line a large roasting pan with foil with excess foil hanging over all sides. Place brisket on foil. Spread half of seasoning mixture on lean side of brisket. Turn over and spread remaining mixture on fat side. Fold excess foil toward brisket, but do not cover.

Broil brisket (with electric oven door partially open) for 5 to 7 minutes or until fat begins to soften and emit juices; remove from oven. Unfold foil and wrap over brisket, sealing well. Reduce oven temperature to bake at 225°. Bake brisket for 12 hours.

fajitas

yields 6 servings

2	(7-ounce) cans salsa verde		garlic salt
1	cup Italian salad dressing		black pepper
3	serrano chiles, chopped	3	pounds skirt steak
2	cloves garlic, chopped		warm flour tortillas

Combine salsa, dressing, chile, garlic, garlic salt and pepper in a shallow container. Add steak, turning to coat. Cover and refrigerate at least 6 hours.

Prepare barbecue grill for high heat. Remove meat from marinade, discarding marinade. Grill meat until desired degree of doneness. Cut into strips against the grain. Serve in warm flour tortillas with desired toppings.

★ poquito mas ★

The beef fajita was born when Mexican cowboys figured out how to cook a cut of meat called the skirt steak, which their boss rejected because it was too tough. The cowboys grilled this cast-off meat over a very hot wood fire, bringing out its robust flavor. Fajitas are eaten by wrapping meat in a flour tortilla. They are served with a combination of different colored peppers and onions, which have been freshly cooked in a lightly oiled pan. Fajitas can be served with a spicy tomato sauce, sour cream and grated cheese.

"no-peek" beef burgundy

yields 4 to 6 servings

2	pounds stew meat	¾	cup burgundy wine
1	(1-ounce) package onion soup mix		dried marjoram
1	(10¾-ounce) can cream of mushroom soup		dried thyme
			black pepper
1-2	tablespoons concentrated beef bouillon		paprika
			dried parsley

Preheat oven to 300°. Combine meat, soup mix, soup, bouillon, wine, marjoram, thyme, pepper, paprika and parsley in a large soup pot or Dutch oven.

Bake, covered, for 2 hours and 45 minutes. Do not peek! Uncover; if gravy is too thick, stir in one soup can of water. If gravy is too thin, stir in another can of cream of mushroom soup. Cover and bake 15 minutes. Serve over rice.

carne guisada

yields 6 servings

¼	cup shortening		1	teaspoon ground cumin
1	large onion, chopped			salt
1	green bell pepper, chopped		6	chiltepin or pequin chiles, optional
3	pounds stew meat		1	seeded and chopped jalapeño, optional
1	(15-ounce) can tomato sauce			
1	clove garlic, minced		½	(12-ounce) can beer
1	teaspoon black pepper			

Melt shortening in a large skillet over medium-high heat. Add onion and bell pepper; sauté until tender. Add meat and sauté until meat appears white in color. Add tomato sauce, garlic, pepper, cumin and salt, stirring until well blended.

Grind chile in a molcajete y tejolete (mortar and pestle); add water to remove from bowl and stir into meat mixture. Stir in jalapeño.

Bring mixture to a boil; reduce heat and simmer for 2 hours or until meat is tender and juice has thickened. Stir in beer; cook until thoroughly heated. Serve immediately with refritos (refried beans) and Spanish rice.

★ *poquito mas* ★

Chiltepin- very hot dried peppers that are tiny, oval-shaped with an orange-red color. Also known as "piquin", "bird pepper", "chile bravo" and "chile mesquito".

Molcajete y tejolete- the Mexican term for "mortar and pestle". The molcajete, or mortar, is a bowl-shaped container. The tejolete, or pestle, is the tool used to grind spices, herbs and food in the molcajete. Usually made from volcanic rock, these pieces are black with a rough texture.

devilish good meatloaf

yields 6 to 8 servings

1	tablespoon salt		½	cup chopped green onion
1	teaspoon cayenne pepper		2	teaspoons minced garlic
1	teaspoon black pepper		1	tablespoon Worcestershire sauce
½	teaspoon white pepper		1	tablespoon hot sauce
½	teaspoon ground cumin		½	cup evaporated milk
½	teaspoon ground nutmeg		½	cup ketchup
2	bay leaves		1½	pounds lean ground beef
¼	cup unsalted butter		½	pound ground pork
¾	cup chopped onion		1	cup bread crumbs
½	cup chopped green bell pepper		2	large eggs, lightly beaten
½	cup chopped celery			hotter 'n hell sauce

Preheat oven to 350°. Combine salt, cayenne, black pepper, white pepper, cumin, nutmeg, and bay leaves in a small bowl; set aside.

Melt butter in a skillet over medium-high heat. Add chopped onion, bell pepper, celery, green onion and garlic. Add Worcestershire, hot sauce and reserved seasoning blend. Sauté until mixture begins to stick, stirring occasionally. Stir in milk and ketchup; cook for 2 minutes. Remove from heat and let cool.

Combine beef, pork, bread crumbs, egg and vegetable mixture in a large bowl. Remove bay leaves. Mix thoroughly by hand. Shape mixture into a 12 x 6-inch loaf and place in a 13 x 9-inch greased baking dish. Bake, uncovered, for 25 minutes. Raise heat to 400° and bake 35 minutes or until done. Serve with hotter 'n hell sauce, if desired.

devilish good meatloaf *continued*

hotter 'n hell sauce

¾	cup chopped onion		½	teaspoon white pepper
½	cup chopped green bell pepper		½	teaspoon black pepper
¼	cup chopped celery		¼	teaspoon cayenne pepper
¼	cup vegetable oil		2	bay leaves
5	tablespoons all-purpose flour		1	teaspoon minced garlic
3	cups beef stock		¼	cup minced jalapeño peppers

Combine onion, bell pepper and celery in a small bowl; set aside.

Heat oil in a large heavy skillet over medium-low heat. Prepare a roux by adding flour, whisking until smooth. Cook, whisking constantly, until roux is light brown. Remove from heat and immediately stir in stock, onion mixture, white pepper, black pepper and cayenne.

Return pan to high heat and cook 2 minutes, stirring constantly. Add bay leaves, garlic and jalapeño. Cook, stirring constantly, for 2 minutes.

firecracker casserole

yields 8 servings

2   pounds lean ground beef
1   large onion, chopped
2   tablespoons chili powder
2   tablespoons ground cumin
1   teaspoon salt
1   (15-ounce) can ranch-style beans
6   corn tortillas, torn into pieces

1½ cups (6 ounces) shredded cheddar cheese
1½ cups (6 ounces) shredded Monterey Jack cheese
1   (10-ounce) can diced tomatoes with chiles
1   (10¾-ounce) can cream of mushroom soup

Preheat oven to 350°. Combine beef and onion in a large skillet over medium-high heat. Cook, stirring occasionally, until meat crumbles and onion is tender; drain.

Stir in chili powder, cumin and salt; cook 10 minutes.

Spoon meat mixture into a 13 x 9-inch baking dish. Layer beans, tortillas and cheeses over meat. Pour tomato over cheese. Spread soup on top.

Bake 30 minutes or until hot and bubbly.

best pinto beans with beef

yields 18 to 24 servings

1	pound pinto beans		pepper
1	teaspoon chili powder		crushed red pepper flakes, optional
¼	teaspoon baking soda	1	pound lean ground beef
1	clove garlic, crushed	1	(10-ounce) can diced tomatoes with
	salt		chiles

Place beans in a large soup pot or Dutch oven; add water 2 inches above beans; let soak 8 hours or overnight. Drain.

Combine beans and fresh water to cover. Add chili powder, soda, garlic, salt, pepper, and pepper flakes. Bring to a boil; reduce heat and simmer, covered, for 4 hours.

Brown ground beef in a large skillet over medium-high heat, stirring until it crumbles; drain. Stir beef and tomato into bean mixture; cook 1 hour.

A slow cooker is great to use. Cook for 6 to 7 hours on low.

jalapeño cornbread with beef

yields 8 servings

1	pound lean ground beef		¼	cup vegetable oil
1	green bell pepper, diced		2	large eggs, lightly beaten
1	(4-ounce) can diced jalapeños, drained		1	onion, chopped
1	cup cornmeal		1	(14¾-ounce) can cream style corn
3	tablespoons sugar		2	cups (8 ounces) shredded cheddar cheese
½	teaspoon baking soda		2	cups (8 ounces) shredded Monterey Jack cheese
½	teaspoon salt			
1	cup milk			

Preheat oven to 400°. Brown ground beef in a large skillet, stirring until it crumbles. Stir in bell pepper and jalapeño; set aside.

Combine cornmeal, sugar, soda, salt, milk, oil, eggs, onion and corn in a large bowl, stirring until well blended. Pour half of the cornmeal mixture into a greased 13 x 9-inch baking dish. Top with meat mixture. Sprinkle evenly with cheese and top with remaining cornmeal mixture.

Bake for 30 to 40 minutes or until golden brown.

Recipe can be divided into 2 smaller casseroles. Bake one and freeze one for later use.

french dip sandwiches

yields 8 servings

2	cups water	1	bay leaf
½	cup soy sauce	1	teaspoon garlic powder
4	whole peppercorns	1	(3-pound) boneless beef chuck roast, trimmed
1	teaspoon dried rosemary	8	French or sourdough rolls, split
1	teaspoon dried thyme		

Combine water, soy sauce, peppercorns, rosemary, thyme and garlic powder in a slow cooker, stirring until well blended. Place roast in cooker and cover.

Cook on HIGH for 5 to 6 hours or until beef is tender. Remove meat from broth and shred with a fork. Serve beef on rolls. Pour broth in small bowls for dipping.

Variations: top with Swiss cheese or sautéed onions.

mexican pizza

yields 4 to 6 servings

1	tablespoon vegetable oil	1	(12-inch) prepared pizza crust
1	cup sliced fresh mushrooms	1	(16-ounce) jar thick and chunky style salsa, divided
½	cup chopped green bell pepper		
1	cup chopped, cooked beef or chicken fajita meat or ham	2	cups (8 ounces) shredded Monterey Jack and cheddar cheese blend
1	(2¼-ounce) can sliced ripe olives, drained	1	cup sour cream shredded lettuce

Preheat oven to 425°. Heat oil in a large skillet over medium-high heat. Add mushroom and pepper; sauté until crisp-tender. Stir in meat and olives.

Spread meat mixture evenly over pizza crust. Set aside ½ cup plus 2 tablespoons salsa. Spoon remaining salsa over pizza.

Bake for 10 to 12 minutes. Sprinkle with cheese and bake 5 minutes.

Combine sour cream and 2 tablespoons salsa. Serve pizza with remaining salsa, sour cream mixture and shredded lettuce.

veal with blue cheese sauce

yields 6 servings

1½ pounds veal scallops
salt
pepper
2 tablespoons butter
1½ tablespoons brandy
1½ cups beef broth

1½ cups low sodium chicken broth
1½ cups heavy whipping cream
1 (4-ounce) package crumbled blue cheese
chopped fresh parsley

Sprinkle veal with salt and pepper. Melt butter in skillet over medium-high heat. Add veal and sauté for 2 minutes on each side until golden brown. Transfer to a serving platter; keep warm.

Add brandy to skillet. Bring mixture to a boil, scraping up browned bits. Add beef and chicken broth. Boil 10 minutes or until reduced to approximately 1 cup.

Stir in cream; boil 12 minutes or until slightly thickened. Reduce heat to medium-low; add cheese and whisk until melted. Simmer for 8 minutes or until mixture is thickened. Season to taste with salt and pepper. Spoon sauce over veal; sprinkle with parsley, if desired.

If sauce is thin, add cornstarch dissolved in water. Simmer until thickened.

veal marsala

yields 6 servings

½	cup all-purpose flour	4	ounces fresh sliced mushrooms
⅓	cup grated Parmesan cheese	2	green onions, sliced
1	teaspoon salt	1	cup beef consommé
¼	teaspoon black pepper	1	cup Marsala wine
1½	pounds veal scallops	1-2	tablespoons fresh lemon juice
¼	cup butter, divided		chopped fresh parsley

Combine flour, cheese, salt and pepper. Dredge veal in flour mixture, shaking off excess.

Melt 2 tablespoons butter in a large skillet over medium heat. Add veal and sauté for 1 minute on each side or until browned. Transfer veal to a plate; keep warm.

Melt remaining 2 tablespoons butter in skillet. Add mushroom and onion; sauté until tender. Stir in consommé, wine and lemon juice. Add veal. Bring mixture to a boil; reduce heat and simmer, covered, for 15 minutes.

Place veal on a serving platter; pour pan juices on top and sprinkle with parsley.

Chicken or venison may be substituted for veal.

roasted leg of lamb

yields 4 to 6 servings

1	(4-pound) leg of lamb, trimmed		salt
3	heads garlic, separated into cloves		black pepper
¼	cup butter, softened	2	cups water
1	cup firmly packed light brown sugar	1½	cups red wine vinegar
1	tablespoon ground nutmeg		

Preheat oven to 450°. Cut slits in meat and insert peeled cloves of garlic. Rub lamb with butter, sugar, nutmeg, salt and pepper. Place lamb in a roasting pan.

Pour water and wine in roasting pan. Cover lamb with foil and bake for 30 minutes, basting often. Reduce oven temperature to 350° and bake until meat thermometer inserted in the thickest portion registers 150° for rare, 160° for medium or 170° for well done.

stuffed venison round steak

yields 4 servings

1	pound venison round steak	3-4	carrots, peeled and grated
	salt	2	stalks celery, chopped
	black pepper	1	onion, chopped
10	slices bacon, divided	1	cup chopped parsley

Preheat oven to 325°. Pound steak with a meat tenderizer on both sides. Season with salt and pepper, and place in a baking pan.

Chop 4 slices of bacon and place in a large bowl. Add carrot, celery, onion and parsley, stirring until well blended. Spoon a generous amount of stuffing on top of steak and roll up, securing with toothpicks. Spoon any excess stuffing on top of steak and on bottom of pan.

Place remaining 6 slices of bacon over top of steak roll. Cover with foil and bake for approximately 1 hour.

jalapeño stuffed pork tenderloin

yields 4 servings

6	jalapeño peppers, divided	2	tablespoons chopped fresh cilantro
5	cloves garlic, minced	1¼	teaspoons salt, divided
1	plum tomato, diced	1	(1½-pound) pork tenderloin
⅓	cup lime juice	¼	cup butter, melted

Seed and chop 3 peppers. Combine peppers, garlic, tomato, lime juice, cilantro and ¼ teaspoon salt in a small bowl.

Butterfly pork by making a lengthwise cut down the center, cutting to within ½-inch of edge of meat; open meat. Place pork between sheets of heavy-duty plastic wrap and flatten to ½-inch thickness using a meat mallet or rolling pin.

Spread pepper mixture over pork; roll up and tie at 1-inch intervals with kitchen string. Place seam side down in a lightly greased baking dish. Cover and refrigerate 8 hours or overnight.

Prepare barbecue grill. Seed and chop remaining 3 peppers. Combine pepper, butter and remaining 1 teaspoon salt in a small bowl. Grill pork for 40 minutes, basting often with butter mixture.

ginger-soy pork tenderloin

yields 6 servings

1	cup sake or red wine		2	tablespoons peeled and thinly sliced fresh ginger
½	cup red wine vinegar		3	pork tenderloins, trimmed
⅓	cup low-sodium soy sauce			salt
⅓	cup balsamic vinegar			black pepper
3	tablespoons thinly sliced garlic		3	tablespoons olive oil

Combine sake, red wine vinegar, soy sauce, balsamic vinegar, garlic and ginger in a large, shallow dish or resealable plastic bag. Add pork, turning to coat. Cover or seal; refrigerate several hours or overnight, turning occasionally.

Preheat oven to 400°. Remove tenderloin from marinade, reserving marinade. Pat pork dry and sprinkle with salt and pepper. Heat oil in a large skillet over high heat. Add pork and sear on all sides. Transfer meat to a baking dish and insert a meat thermometer into the thickest part.

Bake until thermometer registers 170° or desired degree of doneness. Let rest 5 minutes before slicing.

Place reserved marinade in saucepan over medium-high heat. Bring to a boil; reduce heat and simmer for 20 minutes or until the liquid reduces and coats the back of a spoon. To serve, slice the pork into ⅓-inch medallions and top with sauce.

stuffed pork chops

yields 6 servings

½   pound hot or mild bulk pork sausage
½   (8-ounce) package herb stuffing mix
¼-½ cup butter, melted
6   pork loin chops, cut 1-inch thick
      minimum

Worcestershire sauce
seasoning blend or prepared
    barbecue rub

Brown sausage in a large skillet over medium-high heat, stirring until it crumbles; drain thoroughly. Combine sausage and stuffing mix in a bowl. Add enough butter to moisten mixture.

Slice a pocket in the side of each pork chop (or ask butcher). Stuff each chop with an even amount of stuffing; seal with toothpicks. Sprinkle both sides of chops with Worcestershire and seasoning blend. Cover and refrigerate 1 hour.

Prepare barbecue grill for high heat. Grill chops for 30 minutes, turning once, or until cooked through, but not dry.

"plum good" pork chops

yields 4 servings

1	tablespoon vegetable oil	¼	cup dry white wine
4	(1-inch thick) pork chops	2	teaspoons teriyaki sauce
6	plums, seeded and chopped	1	teaspoon Dijon mustard
½	cup plum preserves (not jelly)	2	tablespoons water
¾	cup chicken broth	1	teaspoon cornstarch

Heat oil in a large skillet over medium-high heat. Add chops and brown on both sides. Transfer chops to a plate and set aside.

Add plums and preserves to skillet, stirring until melted. Add broth, wine, teriyaki and mustard, stirring until well blended. Add chops to pan. Reduce heat and simmer, covered, for 20 minutes or until done.

Transfer chops to a serving platter; keep warm. Combine water and cornstarch; stir into sauce. Bring mixture to a boil; boil 1 minute, stirring constantly until thickened. Pour over chops and serve with rice.

For a heart-healthy dish, remove all visible fat from chops and brown without oil in a nonstick skillet. Use fat-free, no-sodium broth.

glazed baby-back pork ribs

yields 4 servings

2	racks baby-back ribs, cut in half	¾	cup ketchup
	salt	½	cup soy sauce
	black pepper	¼	teaspoon hot sauce
¾	cup honey	3	cloves garlic, minced

Preheat oven to 350°. Place ribs in a large, shallow baking dish. Sprinkle with salt and pepper. Fill pan halfway with water. Cover and bake for 1 hour.

Combine honey, ketchup, soy sauce, hot sauce and garlic in a small saucepan; set aside.

Prepare barbecue grill. Remove ribs from dish, discarding liquid. Brush sauce over ribs and grill, basting occasionally, until tender. Bring remaining sauce to a boil over medium-high heat; boil 2 to 3 minutes. Serve sauce with ribs.

Basting sauce is also great with pork chops.

vodka-pepper pasta

yields 4 servings

12	ounces linguine or fettuccine pasta		¼	cup heavy whipping cream
2	tablespoons butter		2	teaspoons cracked black pepper
1	tablespoon olive oil		½	teaspoon salt
½	cup minced onion		¼	cup vodka
2-4	cloves garlic, minced		1	cup diced pepper ham
1	cup seeded and chopped tomato			grated Parmesan cheese

Cook pasta according to package directions; drain and keep warm.

Heat butter and oil in a large skillet over medium-high heat. Add onion and garlic; sauté for 2 minutes or until tender, but not brown. Add tomato and cook for 5 minutes, stirring occasionally, until soft.

Add cream, pepper and salt, stirring until well blended. Cook for 1 minute. Stir in vodka and cook for 2 minutes or until vodka slightly evaporates and sauce thickens. Stir in ham.

Toss the sauce with hot, cooked pasta in a large bowl. Sprinkle with cheese and serve immediately.

peasant pasta

yields 4 servings

8 ounces spiral pasta	1 cup chicken stock
1 pound Italian sausage, cut into ½-inch slices	1-2 (16-ounce) cans tomatoes
1 onion, chopped	1 (10-ounce) package frozen peas, thawed
1-3 cloves garlic, minced	2 teaspoons chopped fresh basil
½ cup chopped fresh parsley	½ cup grated Parmesan cheese

Cook pasta according to package directions; drain and keep warm.

Brown sausage on both sides in a large skillet over medium-high heat. Add onion, garlic and parsley; sauté until onion is tender. Add stock, tomato, peas and basil. Bring mixture to a boil; reduce heat and simmer until peas are tender. (Cooking longer will enhance flavor.)

Toss cooked pasta with cheese in a large pasta bowl; top with sauce. Sprinkle with additional cheese, if desired.

deep dish pizza

yields 6 servings

1	(¼-ounce) package active dry yeast	1	pound bulk pork sausage, cooked
1	cup warm water (105° to 115°)	1	(14.5-ounce) can tomatoes, drained and chopped
1	tablespoon oil	1	(2.5-ounce) can sliced mushrooms or 1 cup fresh, sliced
1	tablespoon sugar		
1½	teaspoons salt	2	teaspoons dried oregano
2¾	cups all-purpose flour	2	teaspoons dried basil
	cornmeal	1	teaspoon salt
3	cups (12 ounces) shredded mozzarella cheese	½	cup grated Parmesan cheese

Combine yeast and water in a large bowl; let stand 5 minutes (mixture should be foamy). Stir in oil, sugar and salt. Add flour, one cup at a time, beating until forming a soft dough. Turn dough out onto a lightly floured surface and knead until smooth and elastic. Place dough in an oiled bowl and cover with a towel. Let rise in a warm place until doubled in bulk.

Sprinkle cornmeal in a greased 13 x 9-inch baking pan. Press dough into bottom and up sides of pan. Let rise for 20 minutes.

Preheat oven to 500°. Layer mozzarella, sausage, tomato and mushroom over dough. Sprinkle with oregano, basil and salt. Top with Parmesan cheese.

Reduce oven temperature to 450° and bake for 35 minutes.

dijon ham 'n swiss loaf

yields 1 (12-inch) loaf

4	cups all-purpose flour, divided	2	tablespoons butter or margarine
2	tablespoons sugar	1½	cups (8 ounces) shaved and chopped ham
½	teaspoon salt		
2	(¼-ounce) packages rapid-rise yeast	1	cup (4 ounces) shredded Swiss cheese
1	cup water	½	cup chopped dill pickle
¼	cup Dijon mustard	1	large egg, lightly beaten

Combine 3 cups flour, sugar, salt and yeast in a large bowl; set aside.

Combine water, mustard and butter in a saucepan over medium high heat. Bring mixture to 125° to 130°. Stir into flour mixture. Add enough remaining 1 cup flour to make a soft dough.

Turn dough out onto a lightly floured surface; knead 4 minutes. Place dough on a greased baking sheet and roll out to a 14 x 12-inch rectangle. Sprinkle ham, cheese and pickle lengthwise down the center one-third of dough. Make 4-inch slices from filling to edge of dough at 1-inch intervals along both sides of dough. Bring strips from opposite sides of dough together; twist, and place ends at an angle across filling. Cover loosely.

Place a large, shallow pan on work surface; fill halfway with boiling water. Place baking sheet over pan; let dough rise 15 minutes.

Preheat oven to 375°. Brush with egg and bake for 25 minutes. Serve warm.

southwest artichoke chicken breasts with jalapeño hollandaise

yields 6 servings

6	boneless chicken breasts		1	(14-ounce) can artichoke hearts, drained and chopped
¾	cup all-purpose flour		1	(8-ounce) package mushrooms, sliced
2½	teaspoons fajita seasoning, divided			cilantro and bell pepper rice pilaf
½	teaspoon salt			jalapeño hollandaise
2	tablespoons olive oil			
3	tablespoons butter, divided			

Place chicken between sheets of heavy-duty plastic wrap; flatten to an even thickness using a meat mallet.

Combine flour, 1½ teaspoons fajita seasoning and salt in a small bowl; dredge breasts in flour mixture, shaking off excess.

Heat oil and 2 tablespoons butter in a large skillet over medium heat. Add chicken and sauté until golden brown and completely cooked. Transfer chicken to a serving platter and keep warm.

Melt remaining 1 tablespoon butter in skillet. Add mushrooms and sauté until tender. Stir in artichoke and remaining 1 teaspoon fajita seasoning. Cook until thoroughly heated.

Place a serving of rice pilaf in the center of each serving plate. Top with chicken breast and artichoke mixture; drizzle with hollandaise.

★ *poquito mas* ★

Perched high above historic downtown Victoria on the 12th floor of One O'Connor Plaza, the Plaza Club offers a distinctive ambience and dining pleasure unmatched on the coastal plains of the Gulf of Mexico. Atop the city's tallest and most imposing landmark, the Club provides fine food, impeccable service and elegant atmosphere. Chef Lalo Varela shares his favorite recipes with the Junior League of Victoria for our cookbook. He has been the chef at the Plaza Club for three years and has worked for many famous restaurants before coming to Victoria.

southwest artichoke chicken breasts *continued*

cilantro and bell pepper rice pilaf
yields 6 servings

1½	cups uncooked long grain rice	¼	cup chopped red bell pepper
2	cups chicken broth	¼	cup chopped green bell pepper
1	cup water	2	tablespoons chopped fresh cilantro
¼	cup chopped onion	½	teaspoon fajita seasoning

Combine rice, broth and water in a saucepan over medium-high heat. Bring mixture to a boil. Add remaining ingredients. Cover; reduce heat and simmer for 15 minutes or until rice is tender.

jalapeño hollandaise
yields approximately ⅔ cup

3	egg yolks		dash Worcestershire sauce
1-2	jalapeños, seeded and chopped		dash hot sauce
1	tablespoon fresh lemon juice	½	cup butter, melted
	pinch salt		

Combine yolks, jalapeño, juice, salt, Worcestershire sauce and hot sauce in the top of a double boiler; bring water to a boil. Reduce heat to low; cook, whisking constantly, until mixture reaches 160° and is slightly thickened.

Gradually add butter in a steady stream, whisking constantly until mixture is thickened and well blended.

crab-stuffed chicken

yields 8 servings

8	boneless chicken breasts
¼	cup butter, divided
¼	cup all-purpose flour
¾	cup chicken broth
¾	cup milk
⅓	cup white wine
¼	cup chopped onion
1	(7½-ounce) can crabmeat or ¾ cup fresh lump crabmeat
1	(3-ounce) can chopped mushrooms, drained
½	cup cracker crumbs
½	cup chopped fresh parsley
	salt
	black pepper
1	cup (4 ounces) shredded Swiss cheese
½	teaspoon paprika

Preheat oven to 350°. Place chicken between sheets of heavy-duty plastic wrap; flatten to an even thickness using a meat mallet. Set aside.

Melt 3 tablespoons butter in a saucepan over medium heat; add flour, whisking until smooth. Cook 1 minute, whisking constantly. Gradually add broth, milk and wine; cook over medium heat, whisking constantly, until mixture is thickened and bubbly. Set aside.

Melt remaining 1 tablespoon butter in a skillet. Add onion and sauté until tender.

Combine onion, crab, mushroom, crumbs, parsley, salt and pepper in a bowl. Stir in 3 tablespoons sauce. Place ¼ cup crab mixture on top of each chicken breast. Fold up sides of chicken to cover stuffing. Place seam side down in a greased 13 x 9-inch baking dish.

Pour remaining sauce over chicken. Bake, covered, for 1 hour. Remove chicken from oven and sprinkle with cheese and paprika. Increase oven temperature to broil. Broil chicken for 2 minutes (with electric oven door partially open) or until cheese melts.

chicken breasts with hot pepper jelly

yields 4 servings

4	boneless chicken breasts	2	tablespoons fresh lemon juice
	salt	1	teaspoon Dijon mustard
	freshly ground black pepper	4	stalks celery, cut into 2-inch matchsticks
¼	cup unsalted butter		
1	tablespoon water	2	tablespoons coarsely chopped celery leaves
¼	cup hot pepper jelly		

Place chicken between sheets of heavy-duty plastic wrap; flatten to an even thickness using a meat mallet. Sprinkle with salt and pepper.

Melt butter in a large skillet over medium-high heat. Add chicken breasts; sauté for 3 minutes on each side or until golden brown.

Tilt skillet and drain off most of fat. Add water, shaking pan to loosen browned bits on the bottom. Push chicken to one side and add celery to the pan. Cook for 1 minute, stirring celery.

Combine jelly, juice and mustard; add to skillet, stirring to coat chicken. Cook for 30 seconds until sauce reduces to a glaze. Season to taste with salt and pepper.

Transfer chicken to serving plates and spoon celery on top. Garnish with chopped celery leaves and serve immediately.

chicken breasts in lemon cream sauce

yields 6 servings

6	tablespoons butter, divided			all-purpose flour
12	ounces mushrooms, sliced		1	cup chicken broth
6	boneless chicken breasts		1	cup heavy whipping cream
	salt		3	tablespoons fresh lemon juice
	black pepper		½	teaspoon white pepper

Melt 3 tablespoons butter in a large skillet over medium heat. Add mushrooms and sauté until tender. Remove with a slotted spoon and set aside.

Sprinkle chicken with salt and pepper; dredge in flour, shaking off excess.

Melt remaining 3 tablespoons butter in skillet. Add chicken and sauté 5 to 6 minutes on each side or until golden brown. Transfer chicken to a platter; keep warm.

Add broth to skillet, scraping up browned bits. Bring to a boil; reduce heat and simmer until reduced to ¾ cup. Stir in cream and lemon juice. Cook over medium heat until slightly thickened. Stir in mushrooms, white pepper and 1 teaspoon salt. Add chicken and simmer for 15 to 20 minutes or until sauce is a medium-thick consistency. Serve over steamed rice.

mediterranean chicken

yields 6 servings

15	sun-dried tomatoes (not packed in oil)	3	large cloves garlic, chopped
	boiling water	2	tablespoons chopped capers
6	boneless chicken breasts	1	tablespoon olive oil
	garlic powder	1	tablespoon chopped fresh basil
	salt	2	teaspoons fresh lemon juice
	black pepper	1	teaspoon balsamic vinegar
2	ounces goat cheese (approximately ½ cup)	4	large plum tomatoes, diced and drained
12	pitted, chopped calamata olives	½	cup torn fresh basil leaves
			paprika

Preheat oven to 375°. Place sun-dried tomato in a small bowl with boiling water to cover. Let stand 2 minutes; drain and chop.

Place chicken between sheets of heavy-duty plastic wrap; flatten to an even thickness using a meat mallet. Sprinkle chicken with garlic powder, salt and pepper.

Combine sun-dried tomato, goat cheese, olives, garlic, capers, oil, chopped basil, juice and vinegar in a small bowl, stirring until well blended. Spread 1 tablespoon mixture over each chicken breast, reserving 6 tablespoons mixture. Roll up and secure with a toothpick.

Combine diced tomato and torn basil in a small bowl. Season to taste with garlic powder, salt and pepper. Place half of diced tomato mixture in the bottom of a lightly greased 13 x 9-inch baking dish. Place chicken, seam side down, over tomato mixture and sprinkle with paprika. Spread remaining sun-dried tomato mixture over chicken and top with remaining diced tomato mixture. Cover with foil and bake for 30 minutes. Uncover and bake for 15 minutes.

parmesan chicken

yields 6 to 8 servings

2	cups dry bread crumbs		black pepper
¾	cup grated Parmesan cheese	6-8	boneless chicken breasts
¼	cup chopped fresh parsley		(2½ pounds)
1	clove garlic, pressed	1	cup butter, melted
1½	teaspoons salt		lemon wedges

Preheat oven to 350°. Combine crumbs, cheese, parsley, garlic, salt and pepper in a shallow dish. Dip chicken in butter and dredge in crumb mixture. Place in a greased baking dish and pour any remaining butter over chicken.

Bake for 45 minutes. Squeeze lemon juice over cooked chicken before serving, if desired.

If using bone-in chicken, increase cooking time to 1 hour.

gourmet chicken breasts

yields 6 servings

2	(3-ounce) jars dried beef	1	(10¾-ounce) can cream of
6	boneless chicken breasts, cut in half		mushroom soup
12	strips bacon	1	pint sour cream
			shredded cheddar or Swiss cheese

Preheat oven to 300°. Line bottom of a lightly greased baking dish with beef. Wrap each piece of chicken with bacon, securing with toothpicks. Place chicken over beef.

Combine soup and sour cream; spoon evenly over chicken and top with cheese. Cover and bake for 1½ hours. Uncover and bake 30 minutes.

pecan chicken

yields 8 servings

1	cup all-purpose flour	1	large egg, lightly beaten
1	cup ground pecans	1	cup buttermilk
¼	cup sesame seeds	8	boneless chicken breasts
1	tablespoon paprika	¾	cup butter, melted
1	teaspoon salt	¼	cup chopped pecans
⅛	teaspoon black pepper		

Preheat oven to 350°. Combine flour, ground pecans, sesame seeds, paprika, salt and pepper in a shallow dish; set aside.

Combine egg and buttermilk in a shallow bowl. Dip chicken in egg mixture and dredge in flour mixture, shaking excess.

Place butter in the bottom of a 13 x 9-inch baking dish. Place chicken breasts in dish, turning once to coat with butter. Sprinkle with chopped pecans. Bake for 30 to 40 minutes. (Do not overcook.)

This recipe is easy to double.

braised chicken in sun-dried tomato cream

yields 4 servings

4	boneless chicken breasts		1	cup dry white wine
	salt		⅔	cup heavy whipping cream
	black pepper		½	cup drained sun-dried tomatoes packed in oil
2	tablespoons oil from sun-dried tomatoes packed in oil		6	tablespoons thinly sliced fresh basil
3	large cloves garlic, thinly sliced			

Sprinkle chicken with salt and pepper. Heat oil in a medium skillet over medium-high heat. Add chicken and sauté for 4 minutes on each side or until golden brown. Add garlic and cook 30 seconds. Stir in wine, cream and tomatoes. Bring mixture to a boil. Cover; reduce heat to medium-low and simmer for 3 minutes or until chicken is just cooked through. Transfer chicken to serving plates. Add basil to sauce; increase heat and boil for 2 minutes or until sauce thickens enough to coat a spoon. Season to taste with salt and pepper. Spoon over chicken and serve immediately.

This delicious chicken dish may be served over hot, cooked pasta.

three cheese chicken enchiladas

yields 12 servings

3	tablespoons olive oil		2	tablespoons chopped fresh cilantro or 2 teaspoons dried
2	onions, chopped		24	(6-inch) flour or corn tortillas
2	cloves garlic, pressed		2	cups half-and-half
4	cups chopped cooked chicken		1	teaspoon chicken bouillon granules
2	(14.5-ounce) cans Mexican-style stewed tomatoes		½	cup salsa verde
1	(4.5-ounce) can chopped green chiles, drained		2	cups (8 ounces) shredded Monterey Jack cheese
½	teaspoon salt		2	cups (8 ounces) shredded cheddar cheese
4	ounces goat cheese (approximately 1 cup)			

Heat oil in a Dutch oven or large skillet over medium-high heat. Add onion and garlic; sauté until tender. Stir in chicken, tomato, chile and salt. Bring mixture to a boil; reduce heat and simmer, stirring occasionally, for 15 minutes. Stir in goat cheese and cilantro.

Preheat oven to 350°. Spoon approximately ¼ cup of chicken mixture down the center of each tortilla. Roll up and place seam side down in 2 lightly greased 13 x 9-inch baking dishes.

Combine half-and-half and bouillon granules in a large saucepan over low heat; cook until granules dissolve. Stir in salsa and pour evenly over tortillas.

Bake, covered, for 10 minutes. Uncover and bake 10 minutes. Sprinkle with cheeses and bake 5 minutes or until cheese melts.

tex-mex skillet chicken

yields 6 servings

1 pound boneless chicken breasts, cut into strips	1 clove garlic, minced
1 teaspoon ground cumin	1 cup instant rice
1 teaspoon salt	1 cup picante sauce
2 tablespoons vegetable oil	½ cup chicken broth
1 onion, coarsely chopped	¾ cup (3 ounces) shredded colby or Monterey Jack cheese
1 small green bell pepper, coarsely chopped	1 tomato, seeded and chopped
	½ cup sliced ripe olives

Combine chicken, cumin and salt, tossing to coat; set aside.

Heat oil in a 10-inch skillet over medium-high heat. Add onion, bell pepper and garlic; sauté for 2 minutes. Add chicken; sauté, stirring constantly, for 3 minutes or until chicken is no longer pink.

Stir in rice, picante sauce and broth, mixing well. Bring mixture to a boil; cover. Remove from heat; let stand for 10 minutes or until all liquid is absorbed.

Sprinkle with cheese; cover and let stand for 10 minutes. Sprinkle with tomato and olives; serve with additional picante sauce.

chicken and dumplings with vegetables

yields 4 servings

3	boneless chicken breasts	3	dashes hot sauce
3½	cups water, divided	1½	cups all-purpose flour
4-6	carrots, peeled and grated	1	tablespoon dried parsley flakes
1	cup finely chopped onion	2	teaspoons baking powder
1	cup finely chopped celery	¼	teaspoon salt
2	bay leaves	1	large egg, lightly beaten
1	cube chicken bouillon	⅔	cup milk
1½	teaspoons salt	2	tablespoons olive oil
¾	teaspoon black pepper	¼	cup cornstarch

Combine chicken, 3 cups water, carrot, onion, celery, bay leaves, bouillon, salt, pepper and hot sauce in a 6-quart soup pot over medium-high heat. Bring mixture to a boil; reduce heat and simmer, covered, for 30 minutes. (You can use frozen chicken breasts. Increase cooking time to 45 minutes.) Remove chicken from pot; shred. Return to pot.

Combine flour, parsley, baking powder and salt in a bowl. Combine egg, milk and oil; stir into flour mixture with a fork to make a very thick batter; set aside.

Combine cornstarch and remaining ½ cup water; stir into chicken mixture. Drop dumpling batter, ⅓ cup at a time, into simmering chicken mixture. Cover and simmer for 10 minutes or until dumplings are no longer doughy and are well set.

This is delicious when served with a green or fruit salad. It is a great dish for families who do not care for vegetables. The finely diced vegetables are well hidden in the sauce.

geanie morrison

This recipe was graciously submitted by Geanie Morrison, the current State Representative for District 30. She has recently completed her first session in the Texas Legislature. Prior to running for office, Geanie served as the Executive Director of the Governor's Commission for Women. She also served on the Texas Commission for Volunteerism and Community Service and the Texas Juvenile Probation Commission, both of which were appointments by Governor George W. Bush. Community involvement has and always will be a very important part of Geanie's life. Her fifteen year commitment to the Junior League of Victoria allowed Geanie to be involved in such worthwhile causes as "Making the Grade" and "Great Expectations," of which she chaired.

chicken spaghetti

yields 10 to 12 servings

4-5   pounds mixed chicken pieces
3   stalks celery, chopped
2   onions, chopped
1   green bell pepper, chopped
2   cloves garlic, crushed
1   (4-ounce) can mushroom stems and pieces, drained
1   (10-ounce) package spaghetti, broken into pieces
1   (10¾-ounce) can cream of mushroom soup

1   (10-ounce) can diced tomatoes and green chiles
1   (4-ounce) can chopped ripe olives
    salt
    black pepper
    paprika
3   dashes Worcestershire sauce
1   (16-ounce) package Mexican-style process cheese spread

Place chicken in a large soup pot with seasoned water to cover. Bring mixture to a boil; reduce heat and simmer until chicken is tender. Remove chicken and broth, reserving broth. Dice chicken, discarding skin and bones; set aside.

Measure 1 quart broth back into pan. Add celery, onion, bell pepper, garlic and mushroom. Bring mixture to a boil; add spaghetti and cook until spaghetti is tender.

Combine soup, tomato, olives, salt, pepper and paprika in a large bowl. Stir in Worcestershire sauce, cheese and reserved chicken. Add to spaghetti mixture.

chicken pasta

yields 8 servings

8	boneless chicken breasts		1	red bell pepper, sliced
	onion powder		1	head garlic, cloves separated and pressed
	garlic powder		1	(7-ounce) jar sun-dried tomatoes packed in oil, sliced into strips
	chili powder		1	(3-ounce) jar capers, drained
	salt		½	(28-ounce) jar plain spaghetti sauce
	pepper		1	pint heavy whipping cream
1	(16-ounce) package penne rigate pasta		1	bunch fresh basil, chopped
¾	cup olive oil		¼	cup freshly grated Parmesan cheese
1	orange bell pepper, sliced			
1	yellow bell pepper, sliced			

Preheat oven to 400°. Sprinkle chicken with onion powder, garlic powder, chili powder, salt and pepper and place in a large baking pan. Bake for 35 minutes or until tender. Cool and cut into pieces; set aside.

Cook pasta according to package directions; drain and keep warm.

Heat oil in a large skillet over medium-high heat. Add peppers and garlic; sauté for 7 to 10 minutes. Add sun-dried tomato and capers; sauté for 2 to 3 minutes, stirring frequently. Add spaghetti sauce and cream, stirring until well blended.

Reduce heat to simmer and add chicken, basil and cheese, stirring until well blended. Cook until thoroughly heated.

Combine pasta and chicken mixture in a large bowl.

This recipe is easily doubled.

junior league tea room chicken noodle casserole

yields 16 to 20 servings

1	(3 to 4-pound) whole chicken	1	(4.5-ounce) can sliced mushrooms, drained
4	bone-in chicken breasts	1	(4.25-ounce) can chopped ripe olives
3	stalks celery, chopped	¼	teaspoon paprika
1	onion, chopped	1	teaspoon steak sauce
1	(8-ounce) package noodles	2	tablespoons Worcestershire sauce
2	(10¾-ounce) cans cream of mushroom soup	6	slices crisp cooked bacon, crumbled
1	(8-ounce) can water chestnuts, chopped, liquid reserved	1½	cups shredded process cheese spread or cheddar cheese
1	(3-ounce) jar dried beef, chopped		

Combine chicken, breasts, celery and onion in a large soup pot with water to cover. Bring to a boil; reduce heat and simmer until tender. Remove chicken, reserving broth, and let stand until cool enough to handle. Chop chicken into pieces, discarding skin and bones.

Discard celery and onion and bring broth to a boil over medium-high heat. Add noodles and cook until tender; drain and set aside.

Preheat oven to 325°. Combine chicken, noodles and soup in a large bowl, stirring until well blended. Stir in water chestnuts, reserved liquid, beef, mushroom, olive, paprika, steak sauce and Worcestershire sauce. Spoon mixture evenly into 2 lightly greased 13 x 9-inch baking dishes.

Bake for 30 minutes. Remove from oven and stir in bacon. Spread cheese over top and bake 5 to 6 minutes.

★ poquito mas ★

This dish was served at the Junior League Tea Room in the early years of the League's existence in Victoria. It came to be known as the Junior League Casserole and credit for the recipe is given to the late Mrs. Patrick (Minnie) Welder, and to Mrs. John Smock. It is delicious served with garlic toast and a green salad. It can be frozen.

texas dove

yields 4 servings

¼-½ cup all-purpose flour	1 (10¾-ounce) can beef consommé
dried thyme	⅓ cup sherry
salt	1 teaspoon Beau Monde seasoning
black pepper	dash Worcestershire sauce
12-16 doves, dressed	1 jalapeño, seeded and cut into strips
2 tablespoons bacon drippings	

Combine flour, thyme, salt and pepper in a shallow dish. Dredge dove in flour mixture, shaking off excess.

Heat bacon drippings in a large skillet or Dutch oven. Add dove and sauté until lightly browned on both sides. Remove dove.

Add consommé, sherry, seasoning and Worcestershire sauce, stirring to loosen browned bits on bottom. Bring mixture to a boil; reduce heat and add dove and jalapeño. Cover and simmer for 1½ hours.

grilled quail

yields 4 to 6 servings

1	(14-ounce) bottle Italian salad dressing	1	teaspoon garlic powder	
6	tablespoons fresh lemon juice	½	teaspoon Worcestershire sauce	
1	tablespoon Cajun seasoning	½	teaspoon hot sauce	
1	tablespoon coarsely ground black pepper	12-18	quail, dressed	

Combine dressing, juice, seasoning, pepper, garlic powder, Worcestershire sauce and hot sauce in a shallow dish or resealable plastic bag. Add quail, turning to coat. Cover and refrigerate 8 hours or overnight.

Prepare barbecue grill for high heat. Remove quail, reserving marinade. Grill for 20 minutes, turning frequently and basting with reserved marinade.

For zestier flavor, stuff the cavity of each quail with a strip of fresh jalapeño and wrap with a slice of bacon, securing with a toothpick. Sprinkle the quail with additional Cajun seasoning and grill as directed above.

This is also an excellent marinade for chicken or any other poultry.

fried turkey

yields 8 servings

1	(24-ounce) bottle zesty Italian salad dressing	2	tablespoons garlic juice
1	cup red cooking wine	1	(10 to 12-pound) whole turkey
2	tablespoons onion juice		Cajun seasoning
		5	gallons peanut oil

Strain dressing, discarding solids. Combine dressing, wine, onion juice and garlic juice in a small bowl. Inject turkey with marinade using a basting syringe. Rub outside of turkey with seasoning. Cover and refrigerate 24 to 48 hours.

Heat oil in a large pot to 325°. Carefully immerse turkey in hot oil; fry 3½ minutes per pound. Let stand for at least 10 minutes before carving.

Cook this recipe outside using a propane burner.

south texas barbecued shrimp

yields 8 servings

6	boneless chicken breasts	1	pound uncooked medium shrimp
9	slices thinly sliced bacon, cut in half		teriyaki sauce

Cut chicken into 1 x 3-inch strips; flatten to an even thickness using a meat mallet. Arrange 1 piece of bacon on each strip. Place a shrimp at one end of the strip, roll up and secure with a toothpick. Place shrimp in a shallow container; add teriyaki sauce, tossing to coat. Cover and refrigerate at least 2 hours.

Prepare barbecue grill. Grill shrimp for 15 minutes, turning once, or until done.

Marinated shrimp may be frozen until ready to cook.

gulf coast grilled shrimp

yields 4 to 6 servings

3-5	wooden skewers
1	pound medium shrimp, peeled and deveined
½	cup bread crumbs
¼	cup butter, melted

¼	cup vegetable oil
	lemon-pepper seasoning
	seasoned salt
	lemon wedges, optional

Prepare barbecue grill. Soak skewers in water to avoid burning. Thread 5 shrimp onto each skewer; set aside.

Place bread crumbs on a flat plate. Combine butter and oil on a plate. Place skewers on bread crumbs, pressing lightly and turning to coat both sides. Dip skewers in butter mixture and sprinkle with lemon-pepper and seasoned salt.

Grill shrimp 4 to 5 minutes on each side or until done, basting with remaining butter mixture. Serve with lemon wedges.

shrimp in garlic sauce

yields 4 servings

2	slices onion
3	cups clam juice
2	tablespoons tomato paste
½	teaspoon dried oregano
2	teaspoons olive oil

1	pound large uncooked shrimp, peeled and deveined
4	large cloves garlic, minced and divided
¼	cup dry white wine
	black pepper

Combine onion slices, clam juice, tomato paste and oregano in a saucepan over medium-high heat. Bring mixture to a boil; cook until mixture reduces to 1½ cups. Strain and discard solids.

Heat oil in a heavy skillet over medium-high heat. Add shrimp and half of garlic; sauté for 3 minutes or until shrimp are almost cooked through. Do not overcook. Remove shrimp; set aside.

Add remaining garlic and wine to skillet. Bring mixture to a boil. Cook for 2 minutes or until mixture reduces to a glaze. Stir in clam juice mixture. Bring to a boil and cook 4 minutes or until reduced to a thin sauce consistency. Return shrimp to skillet and bring to a boil. Season to taste with pepper and serve immediately.

grilled shrimp
with feta, cilantro and lime

yields 4 servings

6	wooden or metal skewers	⅓	cup fresh cilantro, chopped and divided
24	large uncooked shrimp	6	thick red onion slices
¾	cup olive oil	4	ounces (approximately 1 cup) crumbled feta cheese
½	cup fresh lime juice		
6	large cloves garlic, pressed		

Prepare barbecue grill for medium-high heat. Soak wooden skewers in water to avoid burning. Peel and devein shrimp, leaving tail section intact.

Combine oil, lime juice, garlic and 2 tablespoons cilantro in a large bowl. Add shrimp, tossing to coat. Let stand 10 minutes.

Remove shrimp from marinade, reserving marinade. Thread six shrimp on four skewers and thread onions on remaining two skewers. Grill onions for 4 minutes on each side or until tender. Add shrimp to grill; cook 2 minutes on each side or until pink. Do not overcook. Remove shrimp from skewers and place on serving plates.

Remove onions from skewers and coarsely chop. Place reserved marinade in a saucepan over medium-high heat. Bring mixture to a boil; boil 2 to 3 minutes. Stir in onion, cheese and remaining cilantro. Spoon mixture evenly over shrimp. Serve immediately.

spiced shrimp
with apple chutney

yields 4 to 6 servings

1	pound uncooked jumbo shrimp	1	tablespoon chopped garlic
1	tablespoon white or apple cider vinegar	½	cup chopped onion
2	teaspoons salt	1	teaspoon turmeric
2	cups unsweetened coconut milk	½	teaspoon ground cumin
1	teaspoon ground coriander seeds	¼	teaspoon cayenne pepper
5	tablespoons vegetable oil, divided	¼	teaspoon black pepper
1	tablespoon peeled and grated fresh ginger	3	tablespoons fresh cilantro, chopped
		1	tablespoon chopped shallots, optional

Peel and devein shrimp, leaving tail section intact. Combine shrimp, vinegar and salt in a bowl, tossing to coat. Let stand at room temperature for 15 to 20 minutes.

Combine coconut milk and coriander; set aside.

Heat 3 tablespoon oil in a heavy skillet over medium heat. Drain shrimp, reserving marinade. Add shrimp to skillet; cover tightly and sauté 30 seconds. Turn shrimp over and sauté 30 seconds or until shrimp are pink, but not overcooked. Remove shrimp with a slotted spoon and return to marinade.

Heat remaining 2 tablespoons oil in skillet. Add ginger and sauté for 30 seconds. Add garlic and sauté, stirring constantly, for 1 minute. Add onions; sauté for 7 to 8 minutes or until golden brown and tender. Stir in turmeric, cumin, cayenne and black pepper; cook 1 minute, stirring constantly.

Remove shrimp from marinade and pour marinade into skillet. Bring to a boil and add shrimp, tossing to coat. Add coconut mixture, stirring until well blended. Bring to a boil over high heat; reduce heat and sprinkle with cilantro. Serve immediately over steamed rice with apple chutney. Garnish with chopped shallots, if desired.

spiced shrimp *continued*

apple chutney

yields 3 pints

8	cups peeled, cored and diced green apple	1½	cups malt vinegar
		1	tablespoon mustard seeds, crushed
2	cups chopped onion	1½	teaspoons mixed pickling spice, tied in cheesecloth
2	cups golden raisins		
2	cups firmly packed dark brown sugar	½	teaspoon ground ginger
		½	teaspoon cayenne pepper

Combine apple, onion, raisins, sugar, vinegar, mustard seeds, pickling spice, ginger and cayenne pepper in a 4- to 5-quart saucepan over medium heat. Bring mixture to a boil, stirring occasionally. Reduce heat to low. Simmer, uncovered, for 2 hours or until most of liquid evaporates and mixture is thick enough to hold its shape in a spoon. Stir chutney frequently as it begins to thicken to avoid sticking and burning. Spoon mixture into three, 1-pint containers. Cover tightly, cool and store in the refrigerator.

shrimp victoria

yields 6 servings

½	cup butter or margarine
1½	pounds uncooked shrimp, peeled and deveined
½	cup chopped onion
2-4	cloves garlic, minced, optional
1	(8-ounce) package mushrooms, chopped
2	tablespoons lemon juice
1	tablespoon Worcestershire sauce
2	tablespoons all-purpose flour
1½	teaspoons seasoned salt
	dash black pepper
1½	cups sour cream
1	tablespoon chopped fresh parsley

Melt butter in a saucepan over medium heat. Add shrimp, onion and garlic; sauté for 5 minutes or until shrimp is almost tender. Stir in mushrooms, juice and Worcestershire sauce. Cook, stirring constantly, for 5 minutes. Remove from heat.

Stir in flour, seasoned salt and pepper. Add sour cream, stirring until well blended. Cook over low heat, stirring occasionally, until thoroughly heated. (Do not boil.) Sprinkle with parsley and serve immediately over cooked rice or pasta.

This recipe can be easily doubled. Serve with a fresh green salad and hot bread. Great dish to be served at dinner parties!

creamy broiled shrimp

yields 4 to 6 servings

1	pound jumbo shrimp, peeled and deveined	1-2	cloves garlic, minced
1	pint half-and-half or light cream		chopped fresh parsley
1	egg yolk		chopped fresh chives
1½	tablespoons fresh lemon juice	1	cup all-purpose flour
½	cup butter, divided	1	tablespoon olive oil

Combine shrimp and half-and-half in a bowl; let stand 10 minutes.

Combine yolk and lemon juice in a heavy saucepan. Add ¼ cup butter; cook over low heat, stirring constantly, until butter melts. Add remaining ¼ cup butter and garlic, stirring until butter melts. Stir in parsley and chives. Remove from heat and set aside.

Preheat oven to broil with baking rack 5 to 7 inches from heat. Drain shrimp; dredge in flour, shaking excess. Heat oil in a skillet over medium heat. Add shrimp and sauté for 5 minutes. Do not turn. Remove shrimp from skillet and place on a baking sheet. Broil for 5 minutes with electric oven door partially open.

Arrange shrimp on serving plates and top with sauce.

mustard shrimp in potato nests

yields 5 servings

12	ounces peeled and deveined medium shrimp	1	large egg, lightly beaten
2	tablespoons plus 2 teaspoons olive oil, divided	2	tablespoons horseradish mustard, divided
½	teaspoon plus ⅛ teaspoon dill weed	½	teaspoon minced garlic
1½	cups refrigerated shredded hash brown potatoes	⅛	teaspoon cayenne pepper
¼	cup soft bread crumbs		vegetable cooking spray
2	tablespoons thinly sliced green onion	3	tablespoons light mayonnaise
		1	tablespoon dry white wine
			fresh dill, optional

Preheat oven to 425°. Combine shrimp, 2 tablespoons olive oil and ⅛ teaspoon dill weed in a medium bowl; set aside.

Combine potato, bread crumbs, onion, egg, 1 tablespoon mustard, 2 teaspoons oil, garlic and cayenne in a large bowl, stirring until well blended. Spoon ⅓ cup potato mixture onto a baking sheet coated with cooking spray. Depress center with the back of a spoon to resemble a 4-inch nest. Repeat with remaining potato mixture. Bake for 10 minutes.

Spoon shrimp mixture evenly in potato nests. Bake for 12 to 15 minutes or until crust is golden brown and shrimp is cooked through. Remove from oven and let stand 5 minutes.

Combine mayonnaise, remaining 1 tablespoon mustard, wine and remaining ½ teaspoon dill weed in a small bowl. Spoon sauce over shrimp and garnish with fresh dill, if desired.

cheese shrimp marinara with spaghetti

yields 4 servings

1	(26-ounce) jar marinara sauce	¼	cup finely grated Parmesan cheese	
2	pounds uncooked shrimp, peeled and deveined	3	tablespoons dried minced onion	
2	cups (8 ounces) shredded cheddar cheese	2	tablespoons finely chopped nuts	
1	(16-ounce) package spaghetti	1	teaspoon dried basil	
1-2	tablespoons olive oil	¼	teaspoon black pepper	
		¼	cup chopped fresh parsley	

Preheat oven to 450°. Pour marinara sauce into a 15 x 10-inch jelly-roll pan. Arrange shrimp in a single layer on the sauce. Sprinkle with cheddar cheese. Bake for 20 minutes.

Cook spaghetti according to package directions; drain. Place spaghetti in a large bowl and add oil, tossing to coat. Combine Parmesan, onion, nuts, basil and pepper; stir into pasta mixture, tossing until well blended

To serve, place shrimp on top of spaghetti and sprinkle with parsley.

If you would rather use fresh onions instead of the dried, sauté ⅓ cup chopped onion in a small amount of olive oil.

shrimp pasta

yields 5 servings

10	ounces pasta	1	(10¾-ounce) can cream of mushroom soup
2	tablespoons butter		
½	cup chopped green onion	1	pound uncooked shrimp, peeled and deveined
½	cup chopped mushroom		
½	cup chopped celery		creole seasoning
1	(8-ounce) package cream cheese, cubed		freshly grated Parmesan cheese, optional

Cook pasta according to package directions; drain and keep warm.

Melt butter in a large skillet over medium-high heat. Add onion, mushroom and celery; sauté until tender.

Add cream cheese, stirring until it melts. Stir in soup and shrimp. Cook, stirring constantly, for 15 minutes. (Do not overcook.) Season to taste with creole seasoning. Sprinkle with Parmesan cheese just before serving.

This recipe does not work well with low-fat substitutes.

crawfish con queso

yields 10 to 12 servings

1	cup butter, divided	¾	teaspoon dried oregano, divided
1	cup finely chopped onion	½	teaspoon minced garlic
1	cup canned green chiles, drained and chopped	3	cups heavy whipping cream
¾	cup finely chopped green bell pepper	1	cup sour cream
2¾	teaspoons salt, divided	3	cups (12 ounces) shredded Monterey Jack cheese
2¾	teaspoons white pepper, divided	3	pounds peeled crawfish tails
1½	teaspoons cayenne pepper, divided	⅔	cup very finely chopped green onion

Melt ½ cup butter in a large skillet over medium heat. Add onion, green chiles, bell pepper, 1¼ teaspoons salt, ¾ teaspoon white pepper, ½ teaspoon cayenne, ¼ teaspoon oregano and garlic. Sauté for 10 minutes, stirring often.

Stir in cream. Bring mixture to a boil; reduce heat and simmer for 10 minutes, stirring constantly. Add sour cream, whisking for 3 minutes or until well blended. Add cheese, stirring until well blended; set aside.

Melt remaining ½ cup butter in a 4-quart saucepan over medium heat. Add crawfish, green onion, remaining 1½ teaspoons salt, 2 teaspoons white pepper, 1 teaspoon cayenne and ½ teaspoon oregano. Sauté for 6 minutes, stirring occasionally. Add cheese sauce, stirring until well blended. Simmer for 6 to 10 minutes, stirring occasionally. Serve over hot cooked rice or spaghetti.

Recipe can easily be halved.

savory crab cakes

yields 4 to 6 servings

½	cup plus 1 tablespoon butter, divided
1	tablespoon chopped onion
1	tablespoon chopped red bell pepper
1	tablespoon chopped green bell pepper
1	tablespoon chopped yellow bell pepper
1	clove garlic, minced
1½	tablespoons all-purpose flour
⅓	cup heavy whipping cream
1¼	cups bread crumbs, divided
1	pound fresh crabmeat
1	egg yolk
1	tablespoon chopped fresh chives
1	teaspoon dry mustard
1	teaspoon lemon juice
½	teaspoon salt
½	teaspoon black pepper
	chive and caper sauce

Melt 1 tablespoon butter in a large skillet over medium-high heat. Add onion, peppers and garlic; sauté 4 minutes. Stir in flour; cook 4 minutes, stirring constantly. Gradually add whipping cream and cook, stirring constantly, until thick and bubbly. Remove from heat.

Add crabmeat, ¼ cup bread crumbs, yolk, chives, mustard, lemon juice, salt and pepper to sauce mixture. Cover and refrigerate 3 hours.

Shape mixture into patties and dredge in remaining 1 cup bread crumbs. Melt remaining ½ cup butter in a large skillet over medium heat. Add patties and cook until golden brown on both sides. Serve immediately with chive and caper sauce.

savory crab cakes *continued*

chive and caper sauce

yields 1½ cups

1	cup mayonnaise	½	teaspoon hot sauce
¼	cup chopped fresh parsley	2	tablespoons drained capers
¼	cup chopped fresh chives		salt
2	tablespoons minced shallot		black pepper
2	tablespoons fresh lemon juice		

Combine mayonnaise, parsley, chives, shallot, juice and hot sauce in a food processor. Process until pale green and well blended. Transfer mixture to a small bowl. Stir in capers and season to taste with salt and pepper. Cover and refrigerate up to 1 day before serving.

scalloped oysters

yields 6 servings

3	cups cracker crumbs, divided	½	cup butter, cut into pieces, divided
2	(12-ounce) containers fresh oysters, drained and divided	2	large eggs, lightly beaten
	salt	1¼	cups half-and-half
	black pepper	¼	teaspoon Worcestershire sauce

Preheat oven to 350°. Sprinkle ½ cup crumbs in a lightly greased 8 x 8-inch baking dish. Cover with half of the oysters; sprinkle with salt and pepper. Dot with half of butter and sprinkle with 1¼ cups cracker crumbs. Repeat layers with remaining oysters, salt, pepper, butter and cracker crumbs.

Combine eggs, half-and-half and Worcestershire sauce, beating well. Pour over oysters. Bake for 40 minutes or until bubbly and lightly browned.

trout veracruzana

yields 4 servings

1	tablespoon olive oil		1	tablespoon chopped fresh oregano or 1 teaspoon dried
2	onions, chopped		⅛	teaspoon ground cinnamon
3	cloves garlic, minced		2½	cups canned, peeled low-sodium tomatoes, crushed
½-1	jalapeño or serrano pepper, seeded and minced		1	bay leaf
8	large Spanish or Italian green olives, pitted and chopped		1-2	tablespoons fresh lime juice
2	tablespoons capers, drained and chopped if large		1½	pounds trout fillets

Heat oil in a large, nonstick skillet over medium-high heat. Add onion and sauté until tender and light golden brown. Add garlic and jalapeño; sauté for 30 seconds. Stir in olive, capers, oregano and cinnamon.

Add tomato and bay leaf. Bring mixture to a boil; reduce heat and simmer 10 minutes. Cover and refrigerate until ready to serve.

Wash fish and coat with lime juice. Cover and refrigerate no longer than 1 hour.

Heat sauce in a large skillet over medium-low heat. Place fish in skillet, spooning sauce over fish to cover. Measure fish at its thickest part and cook 8 to 10 minutes per inch. Remove bay leaf and serve fish and sauce over boiled potatoes or hot, cooked rice.

Also delicious made with boneless redfish or snapper.

red snapper
with sherry beurre blanc

yields 4 servings

½ cup medium-dry sherry
¼ cup dry white wine or water
2 tablespoons sherry or white wine vinegar
2 large shallots, minced (approximately ¼ cup)
salt

black pepper
6 tablespoons cold, unsalted butter, cut into pieces
4 (½-inch thick) red snapper fillets (approximately 10 ounces total) or any firm white fish

Combine sherry, wine, vinegar, shallot, salt and pepper in a small saucepan over medium-high heat. Bring mixture to a boil; reduce heat and simmer until liquid reduces to ¼ cup. Remove from heat.

Add butter, one piece at a time, whisking until blended. (The sauce should not get hot enough to liquefy the butter. It should be the consistency of thin hollandaise.) Set aside.

Preheat oven to broil. Line a broiler pan with foil and arrange fillets on top. Sprinkle with salt and pepper. Broil snapper 4 inches away from the heat (with electric oven door partially open) for 4 to 5 minutes or until fish flakes when tested with a fork. Place snapper on serving plates and top with sauce.

★ *poquito mas* ★

Beurre blanc- a classic French white butter sauce delicious with poultry, seafood, vegetables and eggs. The sauce is traditionally made with a wine, vinegar and shallot reduction blended with unsalted butter. It is important to vigorously whisk in butter pieces so the mixture forms an emulsion, rather than melting to an oil. Overheating a beurre blanc sauce will cause it to separate.

red snapper
with cilantro-lime vinaigrette

yields 4 servings

¼	cup sugar		1	shallot, finely chopped
¼	cup extra-virgin olive oil		1½	teaspoons finely chopped fresh cilantro
2	tablespoons lime juice			
2	tablespoons red wine vinegar		4	red snapper fillets, or any firm white fish
1	clove garlic, minced			

Combine sugar, oil, juice, vinegar, garlic, shallot and cilantro in a jar. Cover and shake vigorously. Let stand 1 hour.

Place snapper in a shallow dish; add vinaigrette, turning to coat fillets. Cover and refrigerate at least 30 minutes up to 2 hours.

Preheat oven to broil. Drain fish, discarding marinade, and place on a broiler pan. Broil for 5 minutes on each side (with electric oven door partially open) or until fish flakes when tested with a fork.

This marinade is a nice accompaniment with blackened seafood.

flounder stuffed with crabmeat

yields 8 servings

¼	cup plus 3 tablespoons butter, divided
¼	cup chopped onion
1	(3-ounce) can sliced mushrooms, undrained
1	(7½-ounce) can crabmeat, drained, or fresh crabmeat
½	cup cracker crumbs
2	tablespoons chopped fresh parsley
¾	teaspoon salt, divided
	dash black pepper
8	flounder fillets
	milk
3	tablespoons all-purpose flour
⅓	cup dry white wine
1	cup (4 ounces) shredded Swiss cheese
½	teaspoon paprika

Preheat oven to 400°. Melt ¼ cup butter in a skillet over medium heat. Add onion and sauté until tender. Drain mushrooms, reserving liquid. Stir in mushroom, crabmeat, cracker crumbs, parsley, ½ teaspoon salt and pepper. Remove from heat.

Place flounder, skin side down, on a work surface. Spread crab mixture evenly over fillets; bring ends up to center, overlapping slightly and secure with toothpicks. Place flounder, seam side down, in a lightly greased 12 x 8-inch baking dish.

Combine mushroom liquid and milk to measure 1½ cups. Melt remaining 3 tablespoons butter in skillet over medium heat. Add flour and remaining ¼ teaspoon salt, whisking until smooth. Cook 1 minute, whisking constantly. Gradually add milk mixture and wine; cook, whisking constantly, until mixture is thickened and bubbly.

Pour sauce over flounder. Bake for 25 minutes. Sprinkle with cheese and paprika; bake 10 minutes or until cheese melts.

seafood lasagna

yields 6 to 8 servings

8	lasagna noodles		2	(10¾-ounce) cans cream of mushroom soup
2	tablespoons butter		⅓	cup milk
1	cup chopped onion		⅓	cup white wine
1	(8-ounce) package cream cheese, softened		1	pound cooked shrimp, peeled, deveined and halved
1½	cups cottage cheese		8	ounces fresh crabmeat, picked and flaked or 7½-ounce can
1	large egg, lightly beaten		¼	cup grated Parmesan cheese
2	teaspoons dried basil		½	cup (2 ounces) shredded cheddar cheese
½	teaspoon salt			
⅛	teaspoon black pepper			

Cook noodles according to package directions; drain and set aside.

Preheat oven to 350°. Melt butter in a skillet over medium-high heat. Add onion and sauté until tender. Stir in cream cheese, cottage cheese, egg, basil, salt and pepper.

Combine soups, milk and wine in a large bowl. Stir in shrimp and crabmeat.

Layer four noodles in the bottom of a greased 13 x 9-inch baking dish. Spread half of cottage cheese mixture over noodles and top with half of seafood mixture. Repeat layers with remaining four noodles, cottage cheese mixture and seafood mixture.

Sprinkle with Parmesan cheese and bake for 45 minutes. Top with cheddar cheese and bake 2 to 3 minutes or until cheese melts. Let stand 15 minutes before serving.

One (10-ounce) package of frozen chopped spinach, thawed, may be added to the cottage cheese mixture for added color and flavor.

Desserts

texas sheet cake

yields 15 servings

2	cups all-purpose flour		½	cup buttermilk or ½ cup milk and 1 tablespoon vinegar
2	cups sugar			
1	cup water		1	teaspoon baking soda
½	cup butter		1	teaspoon vanilla extract
½	cup vegetable oil		½	cup chopped pecans, optional
3½	tablespoons cocoa powder			cocoa icing
2	large eggs, lightly beaten			

Preheat oven to 325°. Grease and flour a 13 x 9-inch baking pan; set aside.

Combine flour and sugar in a bowl; set aside. Combine water, butter, oil and cocoa in a saucepan over medium heat. Bring mixture to a boil, stirring until well blended. Pour mixture over flour and sugar, stirring until well blended. Stir in eggs, buttermilk, baking soda and vanilla. Stir in pecan pieces, if desired. Pour batter into prepared pan and bake for 25 to 35 minutes or until a toothpick inserted in the center comes out clean. Cool slightly in pan on a wire rack. Spread cocoa icing on top of cake in pan while still warm.

cocoa icing

½	cup butter		1	(16-ounce) package powdered sugar
⅓	cup milk		1	teaspoon vanilla extract
3½	tablespoons cocoa powder		½	cup chopped pecans, optional

Combine butter, milk and cocoa powder in a saucepan over medium-high heat, stirring until butter melts. Bring mixture to a boil. Remove from heat and add powdered sugar, vanilla and pecans, beating with a spoon until well blended.

For a tastier cake, use cocoa powder instead of flour to coat pan.

mexican wedding cake

yields 12 to 15 servings

2	cups all-purpose flour	1	teaspoon baking soda
2	cups sugar	1	teaspoon vanilla extract
1	(20-ounce) can crushed pineapple in juice, undrained	½	cup chopped pecans
			cream cheese icing

Preheat oven to 350°. Grease and flour a 13 x 9-inch baking pan; set aside.

Combine flour, sugar, pineapple, baking soda, vanilla and pecans in a large bowl, stirring until well blended.

Pour batter into prepared pan and bake for 30 minutes or until a toothpick inserted in the center comes out clean. Frost cake while still warm in pan.

cream cheese icing

1	(8-ounce) package cream cheese, softened	¾	cup sugar
		1	teaspoon vanilla extract
½	cup butter, softened	½	cup chopped pecans

Beat cream cheese and butter at medium speed with an electric mixer until creamy; gradually add sugar, beating until light and fluffy. Stir in vanilla and pecans.

taqueria victoria's banana cake

yields 12 servings

3	cups sugar		1	cup sour cream
4	large eggs		4	very ripe bananas, mashed
1	cup butter, melted		3	cups all-purpose flour
1	teaspoon baking soda			powdered sugar

Preheat oven to 350°. Grease and flour a 10-inch Bundt pan; set aside.

Place sugar in a large mixing bowl. In the order listed, stir in eggs, butter, baking soda, sour cream and bananas. Stir in flour, one cup at a time, until just mixed.

Spoon batter into the prepared pan and bake for 45 minutes or until a toothpick inserted near the center comes out clean. Cool cake in pan for 30 minutes on a wire rack. Remove from pan and cool completely. Sprinkle top with powdered sugar.

★ *poquito mas* ★

Cliff and Magdalena Kuykendall founded Taqueria in 1985. Beginning in Victoria Mall, the restaurant was moved to the downtown location in the winter of 1991. The menu consisted of Mexican entrées until an Italian menu was added in 1997. Open for breakfast, lunch and dinner Monday through Friday, and for dinner on Saturday, Taqueria Victoria continues to be the downtown favorite in Victoria.

banana-coconut crunch cake

yields 6 to 8 servings

½	cup flaked coconut
1	cup cake flour
½	teaspoon baking soda
¼	teaspoon baking powder
⅛	teaspoon salt
2	large eggs
½	cup mashed banana (approximately 1 large)

3	tablespoons crème fraîche or sour cream
½	teaspoon vanilla extract
6	tablespoons unsalted butter, softened
½	cup sugar
	rum syrup
	banana chip frosting

Preheat oven to 350°. Butter an 8 x 8-inch baking pan and line the bottom with waxed paper. Butter paper and dust with flour, knocking out excess flour.

Place coconut on a baking sheet and bake for 6 minutes, stirring once, or until golden brown. Set aside.

Combine flour, baking soda, baking powder and salt in a bowl; set aside. Combine eggs, banana, crème fraîche or sour cream and vanilla; set aside.

Beat butter at medium speed with electric mixer until creamy; gradually add sugar, beating well. Beat in flour and egg mixture alternately, beginning and ending with flour. Fold in coconut. Pour batter into prepared pan, smoothing top.

Bake for 30 minutes or until a toothpick inserted in the center comes out clean. Cool in pan on a wire rack for 10 minutes. Run a knife around the edges of the pan to loosen and invert cake onto a wire rack. Remove waxed paper; cool completely. Cake layer may be prepared 3 days ahead, wrapped tightly and refrigerated.

Cut cake in half horizontally and brush cut sides with all of the rum syrup. Spread half of the frosting on the cut side of the bottom layer and arrange top layer, cut side down, on frosting. Spread remaining frosting on top of cake. Cake may be assembled up to 3 hours ahead and refrigerated (covered with an overturned bowl or cake keeper) until ready to serve.

banana-coconut crunch cake *continued*

rum syrup

¼ cup water

2 tablespoons sugar

2 tablespoons dark rum

Combine water and sugar in a small saucepan over medium-high heat. Bring mixture to a boil, stirring until sugar dissolves. Reduce heat and simmer 1 minute. Stir in rum; simmer 1 minute. Cool syrup completely before using. Syrup may be prepared up to 3 days ahead; cover and refrigerate until ready to use.

banana chip frosting

⅔ cup crisp banana chips

1 (8-ounce) package cream cheese, softened

¼ cup unsalted butter, softened

1½ cups powdered sugar, sifted

1 teaspoon vanilla extract

pinch salt

Place banana chips in a food processor; process until coarsely ground.

Beat cream cheese and butter at medium speed with an electric mixer until creamy; gradually add sugar, beating until light and fluffy. Stir in vanilla, salt and banana chips.

banana upside-down cake

yields 6 servings

6	tablespoons unsalted butter, softened	1	cup mashed ripe bananas (approximately 2 large)
1	cup firmly packed light brown sugar	½	cup buttermilk
2	large bananas, sliced	1	teaspoon vanilla extract
1½	cups cake flour	1¼	cups sugar
¾	teaspoon baking soda	⅓	cup vegetable shortening
½	teaspoon baking powder	2	large eggs
½	teaspoon salt		

Preheat oven to 350° with baking rack in lowest third of oven. Combine butter and brown sugar in a mixing bowl, beating at medium speed with an electric mixer until blended. Spread over the bottom of a 9 x 9 x 2-inch baking dish. Arrange banana slices over brown sugar mixture, covering completely. Set aside.

Combine flour, baking soda, baking powder and salt in a small bowl; set aside. Combine mashed bananas, buttermilk and vanilla in a small bowl; set aside.

Beat shortening at medium speed until fluffy; gradually add sugar, beating well. Add eggs, one at a time, beating until well blended after each addition. Add dry ingredients alternately with buttermilk mixture, mixing until just combined. Pour batter over bananas.

Bake for 1 hour and 5 minutes or until cake pulls away from sides and a toothpick inserted in the center comes out clean. Cool slightly in pan on a wire rack. Invert pan onto a serving platter. Serve warm or room temperature.

★ *poquito mas* ★

If you don't keep cake flour on hand, make your own. Place 2 tablespoons cornstarch into a 1-cup measuring cup. Fill with all-purpose flour and sift. The mixture will be equal to 1 cup of cake flour.

chocolate-banana cake

yields 8 to 10 servings

	vegetable cooking spray	4	egg whites
2	cups all-purpose flour	½	cup corn oil
1¼	cups sugar	½	cup water
⅔	cup cocoa powder	1	teaspoon vanilla extract
1½	teaspoons baking soda	1	cup buttermilk or plain low-fat yogurt
½	teaspoon salt	1-2	bananas, mashed
½	teaspoon ground cinnamon		

Preheat oven to 350°. Coat a 13 x 9-inch baking pan with cooking spray; set aside.

Combine flour, sugar, cocoa, baking soda, salt and cinnamon in a medium bowl; set aside.

Beat egg whites, corn oil, water and vanilla at medium speed with an electric mixer. Add buttermilk alternately with flour mixture, beginning and ending with buttermilk. Beat in banana until smooth. Pour into prepared pan.

Bake for 40 to 50 minutes or until cake springs back when lightly touched. Cool in pan on a wire rack. Cut into squares to serve.

whipping cream pound cake

yields 12 servings

1	cup butter, softened	¼	teaspoon cream of tartar
3	cups sugar	2	teaspoons vanilla extract
6	large eggs	3	cups cake flour
1	cup heavy whipping cream		

Preheat oven to 350°. Grease a Bundt pan; set aside.

Beat butter at medium speed with an electric mixer until creamy. Gradually add sugar, beating well. Add eggs, one at a time, beating well after each addition.

Combine cream, cream of tartar and vanilla. Add to butter mixture alternately with flour, beating at low speed just until blended after each addition. Pour batter into prepared pan and bake for 1 hour to 1 hour and 10 minutes or until a toothpick inserted in the center comes out clean. Cool in pan on a wire rack for 10 to 15 minutes; remove from pan and transfer to a serving platter.

Pour glaze over warm cake.

This very moist cake freezes well or keeps up to a week.

glaze

1½	cups powdered sugar	½	teaspoon vanilla
2	tablespoons water		almond brickle chips

Combine powdered sugar, water, vanilla and almond brickle chips in a bowl, stirring until well blended.

cranberry cake with warm brown sugar sauce

yields 12 servings

1	cup sugar	2	teaspoons baking powder
3	tablespoons butter, melted	½	teaspoon salt
1	large egg, lightly beaten	2	cups whole cranberries, washed and drained
1	cup milk		warm brown sugar sauce
2	cups all-purpose flour		

Preheat oven to 350°. Grease and flour an 8 x 8-inch baking pan or 6-cup Bundt pan; set aside.

Beat sugar, butter and egg at medium speed with an electric mixer until well blended. Add milk, beating until blended.

Combine flour, baking powder and salt. Add to butter mixture, stirring just until mixed. Fold in cranberries and pour batter into prepared pan.

Bake for 30 to 40 minutes or until a toothpick inserted in the center comes out clean. Cool in pan on wire rack. Slice and spoon sauce over each serving.

warm brown sugar sauce

1	cup firmly packed light brown sugar	1	cup heavy whipping cream or half-and-half
1	cup sugar		
3	tablespoons butter		

Combine brown sugar, sugar, butter and cream in a saucepan over medium-high heat. Cook for 5 minutes, stirring often, or until sugar dissolves.

$175 cake

yields 8 to 10 servings

1	(18.25-ounce) package devil's food cake mix	1	cup chopped nuts
3	large eggs, divided	1	(16-ounce) package powdered sugar, sifted
½	cup butter, melted	1	(8-ounce) package cream cheese, softened
1	(6-ounce) package semisweet chocolate morsels		

Preheat oven to 350°. Combine cake mix, 1 egg and butter; press into the bottom of a greased 13 x 9-inch baking pan. Sprinkle with chocolate morsels and nuts.

Combine powdered sugar, cream cheese and remaining 2 eggs, beating until well blended. Pour over nuts and bake for 30 minutes or until golden brown. May be served warm.

texas gold bars

yields 8 to 10 servings

1	(18.25-ounce) package butter-flavored cake mix	1	(8-ounce) package cream cheese, softened
4	large eggs, divided	1	teaspoon vanilla extract
½	cup butter or margarine, softened	1	(16-ounce) package powdered sugar

Preheat oven to 350°. Combine cake mix, 1 egg and butter; press into the bottom of a greased 13 x 9-inch baking pan.

Combine cream cheese, remaining 3 eggs and vanilla, beating until well blended. Stir in powdered sugar, beating until smooth. Pour over crust and bake for 10 minutes.

Reduce oven temperature to 325° and bake for 30 minutes. Watch carefully so cake does not burn. Cool before serving.

margarita cake

yields 12 servings

1	(18.25-ounce) package lemon-flavored cake mix	¼	cup water
1	(3.9-ounce) package instant lemon pudding mix	4	large eggs, lightly beaten
½	cup canola or vegetable oil	½	cup gold tequila
½	cup frozen limeade concentrate	2	tablespoons Triple Sec or orange-flavored liqueur
			tequila-lime glaze

Preheat oven to 350°. Grease and flour a Bundt pan; set aside.

Combine cake mix, pudding mix, oil, limeade, water, eggs, tequila and liqueur in a large bowl. Beat for 5 minutes at medium speed with an electric mixer. Pour batter in prepared pan.

Bake for 45 to 55 minutes or until a toothpick inserted in the center comes out clean. Cool in pan on a wire rack for 10 to 15 minutes; remove from pan and cool completely. Spoon tequila-lime glaze over cooled cake.

tequila-lime glaze

1½	tablespoons tequila	¼	teaspoon grated lime peel
1	tablespoon Triple Sec or orange-flavored liqueur	1	tablespoon fresh lime juice
		1¼	cups packed powdered sugar

Combine tequila, liqueur, peel, juice and sugar in a bowl, stirring until well blended. Add more powdered sugar for a thicker glaze.

gingerbread cake

yields 8 to 10 servings

¾	cup butter, softened		1	teaspoon ground cinnamon
1	(16-ounce) package dark brown sugar		1	teaspoon ground ginger
2	cups all-purpose flour		1	teaspoon ground nutmeg
½	teaspoon salt		1	teaspoon baking soda
2	large eggs, lightly beaten		¼	cup buttermilk
			¼	cup molasses

Preheat oven to 350°. Grease and flour a 13 x 9-inch baking pan; set aside.

Combine butter, sugar, flour and salt in a large bowl, stirring by hand until well blended. Measure ¾ cup and set aside.

Combine eggs, cinnamon, ginger, nutmeg, baking soda, buttermilk and molasses; stir into remaining sugar mixture, beating until well blended. Pour batter into prepared pan and sprinkle with reserved sugar mixture.

Bake for 40 to 45 minutes or until a toothpick inserted in the center comes out clean. Cool in pan on wire rack.

★ plum cake

yields 12 servings

2 cups all-purpose flour
2 cups sugar
1 teaspoon ground cinnamon
1 teaspoon baking soda
½-1 teaspoon ground cloves
½ teaspoon salt
1 cup vegetable oil

3 large eggs, lightly beaten
2 (4-ounce) jars baby food plums with tapioca
1 teaspoon vanilla extract
1 cup chopped nuts, optional
   powdered sugar

Preheat oven to 350°. Grease and flour a 10-inch tube pan; set aside.

Combine flour, sugar, cinnamon, baking soda, cloves and salt in a large bowl. Add oil, eggs, plums and vanilla, stirring by hand until well blended. Stir in nuts. Pour batter into prepared pan and bake for 1 hour or until a toothpick inserted in the center comes out clean. Cool in pan on a wire rack to 10 to 15 minutes; remove from pan and cool completely. Sift powdered sugar over cake.

This cake keeps well or freezes. A favorite with everyone.

double frosted chocolate bourbon brownies

yields approximately 6½ dozen

¾	cup all-purpose flour		1	teaspoon vanilla extract
¼	teaspoon baking soda		2	large eggs
¼	teaspoon salt		1½	cups pecans, coarsely chopped
½	cup sugar		2-4	tablespoons bourbon
⅓	cup shortening			white frosting
2	tablespoons water			chocolate glaze
1	(6-ounce) package semisweet morsels			

Preheat oven to 325°. Combine flour, baking soda and salt, stirring until blended; set aside.

Combine sugar, shortening and water in a saucepan over medium-high heat. Bring mixture just to a boil, stirring constantly. Remove from heat.

Stir in chocolate morsels and vanilla. Beat in eggs, one at a time. Stir in flour mixture and nuts. Spread batter into a lightly greased 13 x 9-inch baking pan.

Bake for 25 to 30 minutes. Remove from oven. Sprinkle with bourbon and cool.

Spread white frosting over cooled brownies; refrigerate until well chilled. Spread chocolate glaze over white frosting and refrigerate until firm. Cut into 1-inch squares. Keep refrigerated until ready to serve.

A very good recipe - and different!

double frosted chocolate bourbon brownies *continued*

white frosting

½ cup butter, softened   2 cups powdered sugar
1 teaspoon vanilla or rum extract

Combine butter and vanilla, beating until creamy. Gradually add sugar, beating until smooth.

chocolate glaze

1 tablespoon shortening   1 (6-ounce) package semisweet
                                      chocolate morsels

Combine shortening and chocolate morsels in top of a double boiler; bring water to a boil. Reduce heat to low; cook, stirring constantly, until chocolate melts.

pavlova
fresh fruit in a fluffy meringue
yields 12 servings

6	egg whites	1	tablespoon Kirsch or other cherry-flavored liqueur
1½	teaspoons vinegar		
1½	teaspoons vanilla extract	3	tablespoons powdered sugar
2	cups super fine sugar	1	pint strawberries, hulled or 3 to 4 sliced kiwi or a mixture of both
1	quart heavy whipping cream		

Preheat oven to 250°. Line a baking sheet with aluminum foil and generously grease and flour; set aside.

Beat egg whites on low speed with an electric mixer until soft peaks form. Add vinegar and vanilla, beating on high speed until stiff peaks form. Reduce speed to low and gradually add sugar, beating continuously until thoroughly blended.

Spoon meringue onto prepared baking sheet forming a 12-inch oval or rectangle.

Bake for 1 hour. Remove from baking sheet and let dry on a wire rack in a draft-free area.

Beat whipping cream and liqueur until foamy; gradually add sugar, beating until soft peaks form. Spread whipped cream over meringue and top with berries, kiwi or both.

★ poquito mas ★

For perfect whipped cream, chill beater, bowl and cream before whipping.

texas size cheesecake

yields 12 servings

1	cup graham cracker crumbs
1	cup plus 3 tablespoons sugar, divided
3	tablespoons butter, melted
5	(8-ounce) packages cream cheese, softened

3	tablespoons all-purpose flour
1	tablespoon vanilla extract
3	large eggs
1	cup sour cream

Preheat oven to 350°. Combine crumbs, 3 tablespoons sugar and butter; press into the bottom of a 9-inch springform pan. Bake for 10 minutes.

Beat cream cheese, remaining 1 cup sugar, flour and vanilla on medium speed with an electric mixer until well blended. Add eggs, one at a time, mixing on low speed after each addition until just blended. Stir in sour cream.

Pour mixture over crust. Bake for 65 to 75 minutes or until center is almost set. Run a metal spatula around the rim of the pan to loosen cake. Cool cheesecake completely on a wire rack; carefully removes sides of pan. Refrigerate for 4 hours or overnight before serving.

Top with your favorite fruit topping or chocolate sauce.

mocha cheesecake

yields 12 servings

2	cups crushed chocolate wafers	1½	cups heavy whipping cream, divided
2	tablespoons instant coffee granules	½	cup all-purpose flour
¼	cup butter, melted	1	teaspoon vanilla extract
6	(8-ounce) packages cream cheese, softened	⅛	teaspoon salt
2	cups sugar, divided	¼	cup coffee liqueur
3	ounces or 6 tablespoons espresso, cooled and divided	12	chocolate covered coffee beans
6	large eggs, room temperature	12	sprigs fresh mint

Preheat oven to 350°. Combine crumbs, coffee granules and butter; press into a 10-inch springform pan.

Place cream cheese in a food processor; process until smooth. Add 1½ cups sugar; process until blended. Add eggs, one at a time, and process until thoroughly blended. Pulse in 4 tablespoons espresso and ½ cup cream. Add flour, vanilla and salt, pulsing until smooth. Pour mixture into prepared pan.

Bake for 1 hour and 15 minutes or until cake is set. Run a metal spatula around the rim of the pan to loosen cake. Cool cheesecake completely on a wire rack; carefully removing sides of pan.

Combine remaining liqueur, remaining ½ cup sugar, 2 tablespoons espresso, and 1 cup cream in a mixing bowl. Beat at medium-high speed until medium peaks form. Slice the cooled cake into twelve slices. Garnish each slice with the whipped topping, coffee beans and mint sprigs.

If the cake begins to get too brown while baking, shield the top with a piece of aluminum foil.

apple cheesecake

yield 12 servings

⅓	cup butter or margarine		4	cups peeled, cored and sliced cooking apples such as Golden Delicious or Granny Smith
1	tablespoon shortening			
⅓	cup plus ¾ cup sugar, divided		2	(8-ounce) packages cream cheese, softened
1	tablespoon plus ¼ teaspoon vanilla extract, divided			
1	cup all-purpose flour		2	large eggs
⅛	teaspoon salt		1	tablespoon ground cinnamon
			¼	cup sliced almonds

Preheat oven to 400°. Beat butter, shortening, ⅓ cup sugar and ¼ teaspoon vanilla at medium speed with an electric mixer until combined. Add flour and salt, mixing until crumbly. Press into the bottom of a 9-inch springform pan; set aside.

Place apple slices in a single layer in a shallow baking pan. Cover with foil and bake for 15 minutes.

Beat cream cheese, ½ cup sugar and remaining 1 tablespoon vanilla until fluffy. Add eggs all at once, beating at low speed until just combined. Pour batter into pan and arrange warm apple slices on top.

Combine remaining ¼ cup sugar and cinnamon; sprinkle on apples. Sprinkle evenly with almonds.

Bake for 40 minutes or until golden. Run a metal spatula around the rim of the pan to loosen cake. Cool cheesecake completely on a wire rack; carefully remove sides of pan. Refrigerate for 4 hours or overnight before serving.

Serve with caramel sauce or brown sugar sauce, if desired.

beijing garden's pumpkin cheesecake

yields 12 servings

¼	cup butter, melted	2	(8-ounce) packages cream cheese, softened
1½	cups graham cracker crumbs		
1¾	cups sugar, divided	8	ounces mashed or canned pumpkin
1	teaspoon ground nutmeg, divided	1	tablespoon vanilla extract
1	teaspoon ground cinnamon, divided	4	large eggs
1½	teaspoons pumpkin pie spice, divided		

Preheat oven to 350°. Generously grease bottom and sides of a 9-inch springform pan. Place pan in refrigerator.

Combine butter, crumbs, ¼ cup sugar, ½ teaspoon nutmeg, ½ teaspoon cinnamon and ½ teaspoon pie spice in a bowl, stirring until well blended. Press into the bottom of the prepared pan. Return pan to refrigerator.

Beat cream cheese, pumpkin, remaining 1½ cups sugar, ½ teaspoon nutmeg, ½ teaspoon cinnamon and 1 teaspoon pie spice until smooth. Stir in vanilla. Without stopping mixer, add eggs, one at a time, beating until well blended. Pour batter into prepared crust.

Bake for 48 minutes. Run a metal spatula around the rim of the pan to loosen cake. Turn oven off and allow the cake to cool in the oven, keeping door closed. When completely cool, refrigerate at least one hour before removing rim of pan. Top each serving with fresh whipped cream, if desired.

★ poquito mas ★

Beijing Garden Chinese Cuisine- Jin M. Tang and his wife, Sylvia A. Reyna, founded Beijing Garden on October 11, 1996. They are located at 113 South Main Street in downtown Victoria. Jin, a native of China, is both the owner and head chef. He prepares all of the food fresh at the time it is ordered. Sylvia not only manages the restaurant, but also makes all of the desserts. Cheesecake is the favorite dessert of the Beijing Garden customers.

peanut butter cheesecake

yields 12 servings

1½	cups salted pretzel crumbs	1	cup crunchy peanut butter, divided
⅓	cup butter, melted	3	large eggs
5	(8-ounce) packages cream cheese, softened	2	teaspoons vanilla extract
2	cups sugar, divided	1	(8-ounce) container sour cream

Preheat oven to 350°. Combine pretzel crumbs and butter, stirring until well blended. Press into the bottom and 1-inch up the sides of a 10-inch springform pan. Bake for 5 minutes; set aside.

Beat cream cheese at medium speed with an electric mixer until fluffy; gradually add 1½ cups sugar, beating well. Add ¾ cup peanut butter, beating well. Add eggs, one at a time, beating well after each addition. Stir in vanilla. Pour into prepared pan.

Bake for 40 minutes; turn oven off and partially open door. Leave cheesecake in oven for 30 minutes.

Combine sour cream, remaining ¼ cup peanut butter and ½ cup sugar, stirring until sugar dissolves. Spread over warm cheesecake. Cool completely on a wire rack. Cover and refrigerate 8 hours or overnight. Carefully remove rim of pan.

Great served with chocolate sauce.

mexican lime pie

yields 8 servings

1	teaspoon unflavored gelatin		1	(14-ounce) can sweetened condensed milk
2	tablespoons cold water			graham cracker crust
½	cup fresh lime juice			meringue
2	large egg yolks			lime strips, optional

Preheat oven to 325°. Sprinkle gelatin over cold water in a small bowl; set aside.

Combine lime juice and egg yolks in a small heavy saucepan over medium-low heat. Cook 5 to 10 minutes, stirring constantly, or until slightly thick and very hot. Do not boil. Add softened gelatin to egg mixture; cook 1 minute, stirring until gelatin dissolves.

Place saucepan in a large, ice filled bowl; stir gelatin mixture for 3 minutes or until room temperature. (Do not allow gelatin mixture to set.) Gradually add milk, whisking until well blended. (Mixture will be very thick.) Spread mixture evenly into graham cracker crust.

Spread meringue over filling, sealing edge of crust. Bake for 25 minutes; cool 1 hour on a wire rack. Refrigerate 3 hours or until set. Cut with a chilled knife dipped in hot water. Garnish with lime strips, if desired.

mexican lime pie *continued*

graham cracker crust
yields one, 9-inch crust

2	tablespoons sugar	1¼	cups graham cracker crumbs
1	tablespoon butter or margarine, chilled	1	teaspoon ground cinnamon
1	large egg white		vegetable cooking spray

Preheat oven to 325°. Combine sugar, margarine and egg white in a mixing bowl. Beat at medium speed with an electric mixer until well blended. Stir in crumbs and cinnamon, stirring with a fork until moist.

Press into a 9-inch pie plate coated with cooking spray. Bake for 20 minutes or until lightly browned.

meringue

3	large egg whites, room temperature	⅛	teaspoon salt
½	teaspoon cream of tartar	⅓	cup sugar

Beat egg whites, cream of tartar and salt at high speed with an electric mixer until foamy. Gradually add sugar, one tablespoon at a time, beating until stiff peaks form.

★ *poquito mas* ★

Sprinkle 1 tablespoon granulated sugar over the top of meringue before baking. It will be easy to cut and won't stick to the knife.

margarita cheesecake

yields 10 servings

	vegetable cooking spray	2½	tablespoons Triple Sec or orange-flavored liqueur
1¼	cups graham cracker crumbs		
¼	cup unsalted butter, melted	2½	tablespoons tequila
3	(8-ounce) packages cream cheese, softened	2½	tablespoons lime juice
		4	large eggs
2	cups light sour cream, divided		topping
¾	cup sugar		lime slices, strips of lime peel

Preheat oven to 350°. Coat a 9-inch springform pan with cooking spray. Combine crumbs and butter, stirring until well blended. Press into the bottom and sides of pan; refrigerate.

Beat cheese at medium speed with an electric mixer until fluffy. Beat in 1¼ cups sour cream, ¾ cup sugar, liqueur, tequila and 2½ tablespoons lime juice. Add eggs, one at a time, beating well after each addition. Pour into prepared crust.

Bake for 50 minutes or until the outside 2-inches are set and center moves slightly. Remove from oven; turn oven off.

Spread topping evenly over cheesecake. Return to warm oven for 45 minutes (cake will look soft but will set when chilled). Refrigerate until well chilled. Run a metal spatula around the rim of the pan to loosen cake. Carefully remove sides of pan. Garnish with thin lime slices and strips of peel.

topping

¾	cup sour cream	1	tablespoon lime juice
1	tablespoon sugar		

Whisk together sour cream, sugar and lime juice in a small bowl.

apple-cranberry pie

yields 8 servings

¾ cup firmly packed light brown sugar
⅓ cup all-purpose flour
¼ cup sugar
1 teaspoon ground cinnamon
4 cups peeled, cored and sliced tart apples such as Golden Delicious or Granny Smith

2 cups fresh or frozen cranberries
2 tablespoons butter or margarine, cut into pieces
double crust pastry (page 270)

Preheat oven to 425°. Combine brown sugar, flour and sugar in a large bowl. Add apples and cranberries, mixing well.

Roll out pastry on a lightly floured surface to ⅛-inch thickness. Place in a 9-inch pie plate. Spoon fruit mixture into pie shell; dot with butter.

Roll remaining pastry and place over filling; seal and crimp edges. Cut slits in top of crust to allow steam to escape. Bake for 40 minutes or until golden brown.

★ *poquito mas* ★

To prevent soggy crust when preparing fruit pies, brush the bottom of the pie with soft butter prior to adding filling.

double crust pastry

yields pastry for one, double crust pie or two, 9-inch pies

2	cups all-purpose flour	⅔	cup plus 2 tablespoons shortening
1	teaspoon salt	¼	cup cold water

Combine flour and salt in a large bowl. Cut in shortening with a pastry blender or fork until mixture is crumbly. Sprinkle with water, 1 tablespoon at a time, and stir with a fork just until dry ingredients are moistened.

Divide dough into equal portions; wrap each portion in plastic wrap and refrigerate 8 hours. Keep wrapped in refrigerator until ready to use.

chocolate pecan pie

yields 8 servings

3	large eggs, lightly beaten	2	tablespoons butter, melted
1	cup light or dark corn syrup	1	teaspoon vanilla extract
4	ounces semisweet chocolate morsels, melted and cooled	1½	cups pecan halves
⅓	cup sugar	1	unbaked 9-inch pastry shell

Preheat oven to 350°. Combine eggs, corn syrup, chocolate, sugar, butter and vanilla, stirring until well blended. Stir in pecans.

Pour into pastry shell. Bake for 50 to 60 minutes or until a knife inserted halfway between center and edge comes out clean. Cool on a wire rack.

coconut caramel pie

yields 10 servings

1½	cups self-rising flour
1	cup butter or margarine, melted and divided
1	cup chopped pecans, divided
1	(7-ounce) package flaked coconut
½	cup chopped pecans

1	(8-ounce) package cream cheese, softened
1	(14-ounce) can sweetened condensed milk
1	(12-ounce) container frozen whipped topping, thawed
1	(12-ounce) jar caramel sauce

Preheat oven to 350°. Combine flour, ¾ cup butter and ¾ cup chopped pecans, stirring until well blended. Press lightly into a greased 13 x 9-inch baking dish. Bake for 15 to 20 minutes until lightly browned. Cool completely.

Combine coconut, remaining ¼ cup butter and ½ cup pecans in a saucepan over low heat. Cook, stirring constantly, until lightly browned. Cool completely.

Combine cream cheese and condensed milk; beat at medium speed with an electric mixer until smooth. Fold in whipped topping.

Layer one-third of cream cheese mixture, caramel sauce and coconut mixture over crust. Repeat layering twice with remaining ingredients, ending with coconut mixture. Cover and freeze until firm.

This recipe also makes two 9-inch round pies instead of one 13 x 9-inch pie.

makes-its-own-crust coconut pie

yields 6 to 8 servings

4	large eggs, lightly beaten		¼	cup butter or margarine, melted
1¾	cups sugar		2	cups milk
½	cup flour		1½	cups flaked coconut
½	teaspoon baking powder		1	teaspoon vanilla extract

Preheat oven to 350°. Combine eggs and sugar, beating well; set aside.

Combine flour and baking powder. Stir together egg mixture, flour mixture, butter and milk, blending well. Stir in coconut and vanilla.

Pour into a greased 10-inch pie plate and bake for 45 minutes.

easy fruit cobbler

yields 8 to 10 servings

2	cups sugar, divided		1	quart fresh blueberries or other fruit
1	cup water		1½	cups self-rising flour
1	teaspoon lemon juice		½	cup butter, softened

Preheat oven to 350°. Combine 1 cup sugar, water and lemon juice in a large bowl, stirring until sugar dissolves. Add fruit, stirring until well blended. Pour into a lightly greased 13 x 9-inch baking dish.

Combine flour and remaining 1 cup sugar in a bowl; cut in butter with a pastry blender until mixture is crumbly. Spoon over fruit. Bake for 30 to 40 minutes until the top is brown and fruit is bubbly. Serve with fresh whipped cream or vanilla ice cream, if desired.

amaretto bread pudding

yields 8 to 10 servings

2	tablespoons unsalted butter, softened	1½	cups sugar
1	loaf French bread, torn into pieces	2	tablespoons almond extract
1	quart half-and-half	¾	cup golden raisins
3	large eggs, lightly beaten	¾	cup sliced almonds
			amaretto sauce

Preheat oven to 325°. Grease bottom and sides of a 13 x 9-inch baking dish with butter; set aside.

Place bread in a large bowl. Cover with half-and-half and let stand for 1 hour.

Combine eggs, sugar and almond extract; stir into bread mixture. Gently fold in raisins and almonds. Spread mixture evenly in baking dish. Bake for 50 minutes or until golden brown.

Preheat oven to broil. Cut pudding into 8 to 10 squares and arrange on a decorative oven-proof dish. Spoon amaretto sauce over the pudding and broil (with electric oven door partially open) until sauce bubbles. Serve immediately.

amaretto sauce

½	cup unsalted butter, softened	¼	cup amaretto or other almond-flavored liqueur
1	cup powdered sugar		
1	large egg, beaten		

Combine butter and sugar in the top of a double boiler; bring water to a boil. Reduce heat to low; cook, stirring constantly until mixture is very hot. Remove from heat and whisk in beaten egg. Continue whisking until the sauce has come to room temperature. Stir in liqueur.

dessert enchiladas

yields 12 servings

12	flour tortillas	¾	cup butter or margarine
2	cups cherry or apple pie filling		ground cinnamon
1½	cups sugar		sugar
1½	cups water		chopped nuts

Place tortillas on a work surface and spread pie filling evenly down the center. Roll up each tortilla and place in a single layer in a lightly greased 13 x 9-inch baking dish.

Combine sugar, water and butter in a saucepan over medium-high heat. Bring mixture to a boil. Pour over filled tortillas and let stand for 1 hour.

Preheat oven to 350°. Sprinkle with cinnamon, sugar and nuts. Bake for 1 hour. Serve warm with ice cream or whipped cream.

bananas foster

yields 4 servings

2	tablespoons butter	2	ripe bananas, sliced
¼	cup firmly packed light brown sugar	¼	cup rum
	dash ground cinnamon		vanilla ice cream
¼	cup banana liqueur		

Melt butter in a large skillet over medium-high heat. Add brown sugar, cinnamon, liqueur and bananas. Cook, stirring constantly, for 2 minutes or until bananas are tender. Pour rum into skillet; heat just until warm. Remove from heat. Ignite with a long match or lighter. When flames die down, serve over ice cream.

coffee toffee frozen dessert

yields 6 to 8 servings

1	cup chocolate wafer crumbs	1	(1-ounce) square unsweetened chocolate, melted
2	tablespoons butter or margarine, melted	2	teaspoons instant coffee granules
½	cup butter or margarine	½	teaspoon vanilla extract
¾	cup sugar, divided	4	egg whites
4	egg yolks	3	(¾-ounce) chocolate-covered toffee bars, crushed

Combine crumbs and melted butter; press into the bottom of an 8 x 8-inch baking pan or springform pan.

Beat butter at medium speed with an electric mixer until fluffy. Gradually add ½ cup sugar, beating well. Beat in egg yolks, chocolate, coffee granules and vanilla; set aside.

Beat egg whites at medium-high speed until soft peaks form. Gradually add remaining ¼ cup sugar, beating until stiff peaks form. Fold egg white mixture into chocolate mixture. Spread over crust. Sprinkle toffee bars over chocolate mixture. Freeze 3 to 4 hours or until firm. Cut into squares or slices.

Much nicer presentation when prepared in a springform pan.

grand marnier parfait with raspberries and chocolate sauce

yields 12 servings

sugar syrup
8   egg yolks
1   tablespoon water
1   cup sugar syrup
3   cups heavy whipped cream, whipped

3-4   ounces Grand Marnier or other orange liqueur
chocolate sauce (page 304)
fresh raspberries
fresh mint sprigs

Prepare sugar syrup; set aside.

Lightly grease a 9 x 5 x 3-inch loaf pan and line with plastic wrap or parchment paper; set aside.

Beat egg yolks and water in a large mixing bowl for 5 minutes on medium speed with an electric mixer until well blended. With mixer running, slowly drizzle 1 cup sugar syrup into yolks; beat for 15 minutes until light and fluffy.

Place mixture on top of a double boiler; bring water to a boil. Reduce heat to low; cook, stirring constantly for 5 minutes. Return mixture to mixing bowl; beat for 15 minutes or until cool. Fold whipped cream and liqueur into egg mixture. Pour into prepared pan and freeze for at least 10 hours before serving.

Remove parfait from pan, and peel away plastic. Slice into ¾-inch pieces. Pour a small amount of chocolate sauce onto serving plates and top with a slice of parfait. Garnish with fresh raspberries and mint sprigs.

grand marnier parfait *continued*

sugar syrup
yields 2¾ cups

¾   **cup water**   2   **cups sugar**

Combine water and sugar in a small saucepan over medium-high heat. Bring mixture to a boil, stirring until sugar dissolves. Remove from heat and cool slightly.

★ *poquito mas* ★

There will be some sugar syrup leftover. Dilute it with water to the correct ratio and put in your hummingbird feeder. They'll love it!

cranberry sorbet
yields 10 to 12 servings

1   **cup sugar**   2-3   **tablespoons lemon juice**
1   **cup water**   **fresh cranberry sauce**
2½ **cups cranberry juice cocktail**

Combine sugar and water in a saucepan over medium heat, stirring until sugar dissolves. Let cool.

Combine cranberry juice and sugar mixture. Stir in lemon juice to taste. (Begin with 1½ tablespoons, adding more if desired. If too tart, dilute with a small amount of water.)

Pour mixture into a 13 x 9-inch pan. Cover and freeze. When ready to serve, cut into squares and serve in small bowls. Garnish with a dollop of fresh cranberry sauce, if desired.

black and white crème brûlée

yields 8 servings

8	large egg yolks	1	vanilla bean, split lengthwise
⅓	cup plus 8 teaspoons sugar, divided	4	ounces bittersweet or semisweet chocolate, very finely chopped
3	cups heavy whipping cream		

Preheat oven to 350°. Whisk egg yolks and ⅓ cup sugar in a large bowl, blending well.

Pour cream into a heavy saucepan over medium heat. Scrape seeds from bean into cream and add bean. Bring mixture to a simmer; remove from heat. Gradually whisk hot cream mixture into yolks. Strain custard into another large bowl. Transfer a scant 2 cups custard to a medium bowl. Immediately add chocolate to remaining custard in large bowl. Whisk until chocolate melts and mixture is smooth.

Pour chocolate custard equally in eight, ⅔-cup ramekins. Place ramekins in a large roasting pan. Pour enough hot water into pan to come halfway up sides of ramekins.

Bake for 25 minutes or until custard is barely set in center. Transfer ramekins to a baking sheet and refrigerate for 30 minutes or until tops feel firm. Maintain oven temperature.

Spoon vanilla custard evenly over ramekins. Place ramekins in roasting pan. Pour enough hot water into pan to come halfway up sides. Bake for 35 minutes or until custard is barely set in center.

Preheat oven to broil. Arrange four ramekins on a baking sheet. Sprinkle each with 1 teaspoon sugar. Broil 1 minute or until sugar browns. Repeat with remaining custards and sugar. Refrigerate custards at least 1 hour before serving. (Recipe can be prepared up to 6 hours ahead. Keep refrigerated.)

the perfect flan

yields 6 servings

1¾	cups heavy whipping cream	1	cup plus 7 tablespoons sugar, divided
1	cup milk (do not use low-fat or nonfat)	⅓	cup water
	pinch salt	3	large eggs
½	vanilla bean, split lengthwise	2	egg yolks

Preheat oven to 350° with baking rack positioned in center. Combine cream, milk and salt in a heavy saucepan. Scrape seeds from bean into mixture; add bean. Bring to a simmer over medium heat. Remove from heat and let stand 30 minutes.

Combine 1 cup sugar and ⅓ cup water in a heavy saucepan over low heat. Cook, stirring constantly, until sugar dissolves. Increase heat to high and cook, without stirring, for 8 to 10 minutes or until syrup turns deep amber, brushing down sides of pan with a wet pastry brush and swirling pan occasionally. Quickly pour caramel into six, ¾-cup ramekins or custard cups. Using oven mitts, immediately tilt each ramekin to coat sides. Set ramekins in a 13 x 9-inch baking pan.

Combine eggs, egg yolks and remaining 7 tablespoons sugar in medium bowl, whisking until well blended. Gradually and gently whisk cream mixture into egg mixture without creating a lot of foam. Strain custard evenly into prepared ramekins. Pour enough hot water into pan to come halfway up the sides of ramekins.

Bake for 40 minutes or until centers are gently set. Transfer to a wire rack; cool. Refrigerate for 2 hours until chilled; cover and refrigerate 8 hours up to 2 days.

To serve, run a small sharp knife around flan to loosen. Turn over onto a serving plate, shaking gently to release flan. Carefully lift off ramekin, allowing caramel syrup to run over flan. Repeat with remaining flan.

lime flan

yields 8 servings

1⅓	cups plus ½ cup sugar, divided
½	cup water
4	teaspoons finely grated lime peel
3	large eggs
5	large egg yolks

2	cups heavy whipping cream
1½	cups milk
2½	teaspoons vanilla extract
¼	teaspoon salt
	lime slices

Preheat oven to 325°. Combine 1⅓ cups sugar and ½ cup water in a heavy saucepan over low heat. Cook, stirring constantly, until sugar dissolves. Increase heat to high and cook, without stirring, for 8 to 10 minutes or until syrup turns deep amber, brushing down sides of pan with a wet pastry brush and swirling pan occasionally. Quickly pour caramel into eight, ⅔-cup ramekins or custard cups. Using oven mitts, immediately tilt each ramekin to coat sides. Set ramekins in a large roasting pan.

Combine lime peel and remaining ½ cup sugar in a large bowl. Mash lime peel into sugar with the back of a spoon until sugar is moist and fragrant. Add eggs and yolks, whisking to blend.

Combine cream and milk in a heavy saucepan over medium-high heat. Bring mixture to a boil. Remove from heat. Gradually whisk cream mixture into egg mixture. Whisk in vanilla and salt. Ladle custard into prepared ramekins. Pour enough hot water into roasting pan to come halfway up sides of ramekins.

Bake for 45 minutes or until just set and beginning to color on top. Remove from water; let cool 45 minutes. Cover and refrigerate overnight.

To serve, run a small sharp knife around flan to loosen. Turn over onto a serving plate, shaking gently to release flan. Carefully lift off ramekin, allowing caramel syrup to run over flan. Repeat with remaining flan. Garnish with lime slices, if desired.

chocolate cheese ball

yields one, 4-inch cheese ball

1	(8-ounce) package cream cheese, softened	3	tablespoons cocoa powder
¼	cup butter, softened	2	tablespoons Kahlúa or amaretto
¾	cup powdered sugar	¼	cup semisweet chocolate morsels
2	tablespoons light brown sugar	¼	cup finely chopped pecans

Combine cream cheese and butter in a bowl, beating until well blended. Stir in sugars, cocoa and liqueur. Stir in morsels. Cover and refrigerate until firm.

Shape mixture into a ball and roll in pecans. Serve with graham crackers, cookies or sliced fruit.

mounds bars

yields 2 dozen

2	cups graham cracker crumbs	1	(14-ounce) can sweetened condensed milk
½	cup butter, melted	1	(12-ounce) package semisweet chocolate morsels
¼	cup sugar	1	tablespoon creamy peanut butter
1	(7-ounce) can flaked coconut		

Preheat oven to 350°. Combine crumbs, butter and sugar in a large bowl, stirring until crumbly. Press into the bottom of a 13 x 9-inch baking dish. Bake for 10 to 12 minutes; cool.

Combine coconut and condensed milk; spread on top of cooled crust. Bake for 12 to 15 minutes; cool.

Combine chocolate morsels and peanut butter in a heavy saucepan over low heat. Cook, stirring constantly, until melted and smooth. Spread on top of coconut mixture. Cool and cut into bars.

raspberry-oatmeal bars

yields 2 dozen

1	(18.25-ounce) package yellow cake mix	2	cups (12 ounces) raspberry preserves or jam
2½	cups quick-cooking oats	1	tablespoon water
¾	cup butter or margarine, melted	½	teaspoon ground cinnamon

Preheat oven to 375°. Combine cake mix and oats in a large bowl, stirring until blended. Add butter, stirring until crumbly. Press half (approximately 3 cups) into the bottom of a greased 13 x 9-inch baking dish.

Combine preserves and water, stirring until blended. Spread over crumb mixture. Combine remaining crumb mixture and cinnamon; sprinkle on top of preserves, pressing down.

Bake for 18 to 23 minutes or until top is light brown. Cool on a wire rack and cut into bars.

Apricot, blackberry or strawberry preserves may be substituted.

pumpkin cake bars

yields 2 dozen

4	large eggs, lightly beaten		1	teaspoon ground cinnamon
2	cups cooked pumpkin or 1 (16-ounce) can		½	teaspoon ground cloves
1½	cups sugar		1	(18.25-ounce) package yellow cake mix
¼	teaspoon salt		½	cup butter, melted
1	teaspoon ground ginger		1	cup chopped pecans, optional

Preheat oven to 325°. Combine eggs, pumpkin, sugar, salt, ginger, cinnamon and cloves in a bowl, stirring until well blended. Pour into a greased 13 x 9-inch baking dish. Sprinkle cake mix evenly over pumpkin mixture. Drizzle with melted butter and sprinkle with pecans.

Bake for 1 hour and 25 minutes. Cover with foil during the first 30 minutes of baking to avoid overbrowning. Cool on a wire rack; cut into bars. Serve with fresh whipped cream, if desired.

frosted almond bars

yields 32 bars

- 1 cup plus 1 tablespoon butter or margarine, softened and divided
- 1 cup firmly packed light brown sugar
- 2 cups all-purpose flour
- 1½ tablespoons instant coffee granules
- ½ teaspoon baking powder
- ¼ teaspoon salt
- 1 cup crushed English toffee-flavored candy bars
- 2 (2-ounce) packages slivered almonds, toasted
- 1 cup sifted powdered sugar
- 2 tablespoons milk
- 1 teaspoon vanilla extract
- 2 (1-ounce) squares semisweet chocolate

Preheat oven to 350°. Beat 1 cup butter at medium speed with an electric mixer until creamy; gradually add brown sugar, beating well. Combine flour, coffee granules, baking powder and salt; add to butter mixture, beating just until blended. Stir in crushed candy bars and almonds. Spread mixture into a greased 15 x 10-inch jelly-roll pan.

Bake for 18 minutes or until lightly browned. Combine powdered sugar, milk, vanilla and remaining 1 tablespoon butter; spread over warm, uncut bars. Let cool in pan on a wire rack. Cut into bars.

Place chocolate in a resealable plastic bag; seal. Immerse bag in hot water, squeezing until chocolate melts. Snip a tiny hole in corner of bag; drizzle chocolate over bars.

hidden candy cookies

yields 7 dozen

1	cup butter or margarine, softened		1	teaspoon baking powder
1	cup peanut butter		1	teaspoon baking soda
1	cup sugar		½	teaspoon salt
1	cup firmly packed light brown sugar		2	(13-ounce) packages miniature chocolate-coated caramel-peanut nougat bar
2	large eggs			
2	teaspoons vanilla extract			
3½	cups all-purpose flour			

Beat butter and peanut butter at medium speed with an electric mixer until creamy; gradually add sugars, beating well. Add eggs and vanilla, beating well. Set aside.

Combine flour, baking powder, baking soda and salt; gradually add to butter mixture, beating just until blended. Cover and refrigerate until firm.

Wrap approximately 1 tablespoon dough around each piece of candy. Place on ungreased baking sheets and bake 12 to 15 minutes.

lemon cookies

yields 13 to 14 dozen

1	cup butter or margarine, softened	2	teaspoons lemon extract
1	cup sugar	5	cups all-purpose flour
1	cup vegetable oil	2	teaspoons cream of tartar
1	cup powdered sugar	1	teaspoon salt
2	large eggs, lightly beaten	1	teaspoon baking soda

Preheat oven to 350°. Beat butter at medium speed with an electric mixer until creamy; gradually add sugar, beating well. Beat in oil, powdered sugar, eggs and lemon extract.

Combine flour, cream of tartar, salt and baking soda; gradually add to butter mixture, beating just until blended.

Roll dough into 1-inch balls and place on ungreased baking sheets. Flatten each cookie with the bottom of a drinking glass. Bake for 10 to 12 minutes or until very lightly browned.

Vanilla or almond extract may be substituted for lemon extract.

chewy gingersnaps

yields 4 to 5 dozen

¾	cup unsalted butter, melted		1	teaspoon baking soda
1⅓	cups sugar, divided		¾	teaspoon ground ginger
¼	cup unsulfered molasses		¾	teaspoon ground cinnamon
1	large egg, lightly beaten		½	teaspoon salt
2	cups all-purpose flour		½	teaspoon ground cloves

Combine butter, 1 cup sugar, molasses and egg in a medium mixing bowl, mixing well; set aside.

Combine flour, baking soda, ginger, cinnamon, salt and cloves; gradually add to butter mixture, beating just until blended (dough will be soft and sticky). Cover and refrigerate several hours.

Preheat oven to 375°. Roll dough into 1-inch balls and roll in remaining ⅓ cup sugar. Place 2 inches apart on baking sheets and bake for 8 to 10 minutes. Remove from oven and let cool on pans for 1 minute. Transfer to wire racks and cool completely.

melted candy bar cookies

yields 3 dozen

½	cup shortening	1	teaspoon salt
1	cup butter, softened and divided	1	teaspoon baking soda
1	cup sugar	3	cups oats
1	cup firmly packed light brown sugar	3	chocolate-covered caramel nougat candy bars, cut into pieces
2	large eggs	2	cups powdered sugar
1	teaspoon vanilla	2	tablespoons milk
1½	cups all-purpose flour		

Preheat oven to 350°. Beat shortening and ½ cup butter at medium speed with an electric mixer until creamy; gradually add sugars, beating well. Beat in eggs and vanilla.

Combine flour, salt and baking soda; gradually add to butter mixture, beating well. Stir in oats. Drop by large spoonfuls onto baking sheets. Bake for 10 minutes. Cool on wire racks.

Combine remaining ½ cup butter, candy bar pieces, powdered sugar and milk in top of a double boiler; bring water to a boil. Reduce heat to low; cook, stirring constantly, until mixture is smooth. Drizzle over cooled cookies.

texas pecan crunch cookies

yields 7 dozen

1	cup butter, softened		1	teaspoon salt
1	cup sugar		1	cup vegetable oil
1	cup firmly packed light brown sugar		1	cup oats
1	large egg		1	cup crushed cornflakes
1	teaspoon vanilla extract		½	cup flaked coconut
3½	cups all-purpose flour		½	cup chopped pecans
1	teaspoon baking soda			

Beat butter at medium speed with an electric mixer until creamy; gradually add sugars, beating well. Beat in egg and vanilla.

Combine flour, baking soda and salt. Add flour mixture to butter mixture alternately with oil. Stir in oats, cornflakes, coconut and pecans.

Drop by teaspoonfuls (or use a small ice cream scoop) onto ungreased baking sheets. Dip fork in water and press down on each cookie.

Bake for 10 to 12 minutes or until brown. Let cool on pan for 1 minute; transfer to paper towels to drain. Store in an airtight container. These cookies do not freeze well.

sweet ramona cookies

yields 7 dozen

1   cup butter or margarine, softened
1   cup canola or vegetable oil
1   cup sugar
1   cup firmly packed light brown sugar
1   large egg
1   teaspoon vanilla extract
3½ cups all-purpose flour
1   teaspoon baking soda

1   teaspoon cream of tartar
1   teaspoon salt
1   (12-ounce) package semisweet chocolate morsels
1   cup oats
½   cup flaked coconut
½   cup chopped nuts

Preheat oven to 350°. Beat butter and oil at medium speed with an electric mixer until creamy; gradually add sugars, beating well. Beat in egg and vanilla.

Combine flour, baking soda, cream of tartar and salt; gradually add to butter mixture, beating well. Stir in chocolate morsels, oats, coconut and nuts.

Drop by spoonfuls onto baking sheets. Bake for 8 to 10 minutes. Cool on wire racks.

patience

yields approximately 4 dozen

4	cups sugar, divided	2	teaspoons vanilla extract
1	cup milk	2-3	cups walnut or pecan pieces, optional
6	tablespoons butter		

Heat 1 cup sugar in a cast iron or heavy skillet over medium heat. Cook, stirring constantly, until completely melted and golden brown. (Do not burn.) Remove from heat.

Combine remaining 3 cups sugar and milk in a 4-quart saucepan over medium-high heat. Bring mixture to a boil. Stir in melted, brown sugar slowly to avoid boiling over. (The browned sugar must be added to a hot liquid or it will harden if poured into a cold mixture.)

Reduce heat to low; cook to soft ball stage (234° to 240°). Add butter and vanilla; beat with a wooden spoon until cool. Stir in nuts. Drop by spoonfuls onto waxed paper or spread on a baking sheet. Cool completely and cut into squares.

★ *poquito mas* ★

Soft ball stage – if a candy thermometer is unavailable, you can check the soft ball stage the old fashioned way— by using cold water. Candy forms a ball when dropped in cold water and will flatten when removed from the water.

chocolate fudge

yields approximately 4 dozen

4	cups sugar		½	cup butter or margarine
¼	cup cocoa powder		1	teaspoon vanilla extract
⅔	cup light corn syrup		2	cups pecan pieces, optional
2	cups milk			

Combine sugar, cocoa, corn syrup and milk in a heavy saucepan; cook over low heat, stirring gently, until sugar dissolves. Cover and cook over medium heat 2 to 3 minutes to wash down sugar crystals from the sides of the pan. Uncover and cook, stirring occasionally, until mixture reaches the soft ball stage or registers 240° on a candy thermometer.

Remove mixture from heat and stir in butter and vanilla. Cool for 20 minutes or until lukewarm (110°). Beat with a wooden spoon or an electric mixer until thick. Stir in pecans. Drop by spoonfuls onto waxed paper or spread into a buttered 13 x 9-inch pan. (If omitting nuts, use a 9 x 9-inch pan.) Cool completely and cut into squares.

★ poquito mas ★

The history of these two recipes, Patience and Chocolate Fudge, dates back to the street carnivals called Frontier Festivals. These events were the fund-raisers manned by the League's members from 1942 to 1949. The streets were closed to all traffic around the DeLeon Plaza and members staffed the booths for all events. The candy sales and cake walk booth were popular events and the ladies were not hesitant to do their best to attract all the Victoria folk who vied for their creations.

The candy booth was a popular event even during the war. Since sugar was a rationed commodity, ration stamps were saved, donated, and pooled to the cooks who made at least 50 pounds of each variety. The young men stationed at the airbases clamored for this rare taste of home cooking and were willing to buy it piece by piece.

These recipes come from the recipe books of charter members Willy Tarkington and Lucile Pool.

buckeyes

yields 4 dozen

1	(16-ounce) container peanut butter	8	ounces semisweet chocolate morsels
1	cup butter or margarine, softened	⅓	bar paraffin
1½	pounds powdered sugar		

Combine peanut butter, butter and sugar in a large mixing bowl, beating on low speed with an electric mixer, then high speed until well blended. Shape mixture into 1-inch balls. Refrigerate until firm.

Combine morsels and paraffin in the top of a double boiler; bring water to a boil. Reduce heat to low; cook, stirring constantly, until mixture completely melts.

Insert a toothpick into peanut butter balls and dip in chocolate mixture. Place on waxed paper, removing toothpick. Refrigerate until set.

coffee pralines

yields approximately 4 dozen

1½	cups pecan pieces		½	cup milk
6	tablespoons butter		1	tablespoon instant coffee granules
1½	cups sugar		1	teaspoon vanilla extract
¾	cup firmly packed light brown sugar			

Preheat oven to 275°. Place pecans on baking sheet. Bake for 20 to 25 minutes or until slightly brown.

Melt butter in a large saucepan over medium-high heat. Add pecans, sugar, brown sugar, milk, coffee and vanilla, stirring until well blended. Cook over low heat, stirring gently, until sugar dissolves. Cover and cook over medium heat 2 to 3 minutes to wash down sugar crystals from sides of pan. Uncover and cook to soft ball stage (234° to 240°), stirring constantly.

Remove from heat. Beat with a wooden spoon just until mixture begins to thicken. Working quickly, drop by spoonfuls onto buttered waxed paper; let cool until set.

rainbow sweets

yields approximately 4 dozen

1	(24-ounce) package almond bark or white coating		2	cups roasted peanuts
2	cups fruit-flavored round cereal		2	cups pretzel sticks, broken into pieces

Melt coating according to package directions. Combine coating, cereal, peanuts and pretzels, stirring until coated.

Drop by spoonfuls (2- to 3-inches) onto waxed paper; cool. Store in an airtight container.

junior league bon bons

yields approximately 5 dozen

½	cup butter	1	(7-ounce) can flaked coconut
1	(14-ounce) can sweetened condensed milk	2	cups finely chopped pecans
2	(16-ounce) boxes powdered sugar	1	(12-ounce) package semisweet chocolate morsels
⅛	teaspoon salt	⅓	bar paraffin

Melt butter in a large saucepan over medium heat; stir in milk. Add sugar and salt, stirring until well blended. Stir in coconut and pecans, blending well. If necessary, refrigerate until firm enough to handle. Shape mixture into 1-inch balls and refrigerate until firm.

Combine morsels and paraffin in the top of a double boiler; bring water to a boil. Reduce heat to low; cook, stirring constantly, until mixture completely melts.

Insert a toothpick into balls and dip in chocolate mixture. Place on waxed paper, removing toothpick. Cool until set.

★ poquito mas ★

If you do not have sweetened condensed milk, this recipe makes the equivalent of one 14-ounce can.

1	cup powdered milk	⅓	cup boiling water
⅔	cup sugar	3	tablespoons butter, melted

Combine milk, sugar, water and butter in a blender. Process until well blended. This recipe makes the equivalent of one 14-ounce can.

texas millionaires

yields approximately 4 dozen

2   cups semisweet chocolate morsels
2   cups butterscotch morsels

2   cups dry-roasted, lightly salted peanuts
2   cups shoestring potatoes

Combine morsels in top of a double boiler; bring water to a boil. Reduce heat to low; cook, stirring constantly, until morsels are melted and smooth.

Remove from heat; stir in peanuts and potatoes. Drop by spoonfuls onto waxed paper. Let set for 30 to 45 minutes. Store in an airtight container.

sticky finger popcorn

yields approximately 6 cups

1   (3.5-ounce) bag plain microwave popcorn
¼   cup butter

¾   cup sugar
⅓   cup evaporated milk
½   teaspoon vanilla or almond extract

Cook popcorn according to package directions. Place in a large bowl; cool.

Combine butter, sugar, milk and extract in a saucepan over medium heat. Cook for 3 minutes or until butter and sugar melts and mixture is smooth. Immediately pour over popcorn, stirring until well blended.

Drop by large spoonfuls onto waxed paper; let cool. Store in an airtight container.

Tex-cetera

Helpful Hints

cinnamon spice pecans

yields 4 cups

4	cups pecan halves		1	teaspoon ground cinnamon
6	tablespoons butter, melted		½	cup firmly packed light brown sugar
4	teaspoons chili powder			

Preheat oven to 350°. Combine pecans and butter in a large bowl, tossing until coated. Sprinkle with chili powder and cinnamon; stir. Add brown sugar, tossing until coated.

Spread pecans on a baking sheet, spooning remaining sugar mixture from bowl over pecans. Bake for 20 minutes until the nuts begin to brown and sugar melts. Cool and store in an airtight container.

honey pecans

yields 2 cups

2	cups pecan halves		2	tablespoons butter, melted
2	tablespoons honey			seasoned salt
2	tablespoons apple cider vinegar			

Preheat oven to 200°. Combine pecans, honey and vinegar in a large jar; gently shake until pecans are well coated; drain.

Spread pecans on a 15 x 10-inch jelly-roll pan. Bake for 2 hours, stirring occasionally.

Drizzle butter over pecans; sprinkle with seasoned salt and stir well. Bake 1 hour, stirring occasionally.

spicy hot pickles

yields 1 gallon

1	(1-gallon) jar sliced dill pickles	5	cloves garlic, sliced
1	(5-pound) bag sugar	1	(2-ounce) bottle hot sauce

Drain liquid from pickles and discard. Layer sugar, garlic and pickles in three or four layers in the empty jar. Pour hot sauce over top. Secure lid; rotate the jar from top to bottom every day for 1 week.

tropical tomato salsa

yields 2 cups

2	tablespoons lime juice	1	cup chopped tomato
¼	teaspoon salt	¼	cup chopped fresh cilantro
¼	teaspoon black pepper	2	tablespoons chopped shallots
¼	teaspoon peeled and grated fresh ginger	2	teaspoons seeded and minced jalapeño
1	cup peeled and diced mango		

Combine juice, salt, pepper and ginger in a medium bowl. Add mango, tomato, cilantro, shallot and jalapeño, tossing gently until well blended. Serve with grilled fish or poultry.

salsa ranchero

yields 2 cups

2	cups peeled, seeded and chopped tomato	1	teaspoon seeded and minced jalapeño
⅓	cup chopped green onion	⅛	teaspoon salt
2	tablespoons minced fresh cilantro	⅛	teaspoon black pepper
2	tablespoons chopped canned green chiles	2	cloves garlic, minced
2	tablespoons fresh lime juice		dash ground cumin

Combine tomato, onion, cilantro, chiles, juice, jalapeño, salt, pepper, garlic and cumin in a large bowl, stirring until well blended. Serve with tortilla chips, grilled meat or poultry.

blue cheese salad dressing

yields 6½ cups

1	(32-ounce) jar mayonnaise	1	tablespoon prepared mustard
1	(12-ounce) bottle Italian salad dressing	1	teaspoon garlic powder
1	(8-ounce) package crumbled blue cheese, room temperature	1	teaspoon black pepper
		¼	cup chopped fresh parsley

Spoon mayonnaise into a large bowl; slowly whisk in dressing. Add cheese, mustard, garlic powder and pepper, stirring until well blended. Stir in parsley. Cover and store in the refrigerator. Serve on a salad, vegetable platter, or with buffalo wings.

blender caesar salad dressing

yields approximately 3 cups

6	cloves garlic, peeled	4-8	anchovies with capers, or to taste
1	tablespoon dry mustard	6	tablespoons red wine vinegar
1	tablespoon Worcestershire sauce	2	cups extra-virgin olive oil
3	tablespoons fresh lemon juice	1⅓	cups grated Romano cheese

Place all ingredients in a blender in the order listed; blend well. Cover and store in the refrigerator up to 3 days.

hot pepper-cranberry jelly

yields 8, half-pint jars

1	cup chopped jalapeño	1	(3-ounce) package liquid fruit pectin (Do not use powdered pectin.)
3	cups cranberry juice cocktail		red food coloring, optional
7	cups sugar		
1	cup vinegar		

Combine pepper and juice in the container of a blender. Process until peppers are finely chopped. Strain into a large, non-aluminum saucepan.

Bring to a rolling boil. Add sugar, stirring constantly; boil 1 minute. Remove from heat and stir in vinegar and pectin. Stir in a small amount of food coloring, if desired.

Pour jelly into hot, sterilized jars quickly, filling to ¼-inch from the top; wipe jar rims. Cover at once with metal lids, and screw on bands. Process in boiling water bath for 15 minutes to seal lids.

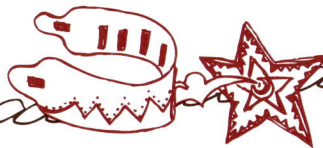

margarita jelly

yields 8, half-pint jars

3	teaspoons grated lime peel	1	(1¾-ounce) package powdered fruit pectin
2	teaspoons lime peelings	4½	cups sugar
1½	cups fresh lime juice	¼	cup tequila
½	cup fresh orange juice		
1	cup water		

Combine juices, water and pectin in a large, non-aluminum saucepan over medium-high heat. Bring to a rolling boil. Add sugar, stirring constantly; boil 1 minute. Remove from heat and stir in tequila and grated peel.

Place some lime peelings in eight half-pint jars and pour jelly over the top, leaving ¼-inch headspace. Cover and cool to room temperature. Store in the refrigerator. Serve with cream cheese and crackers.

If preserving, sterilize jars and lids before filling. Pour jelly into hot, sterilized jars quickly, filling to ¼-inch from the top; wipe jar rims. Cover at once with metal lids, and screw on bands. Process in boiling water bath for 15 minutes to seal lids.

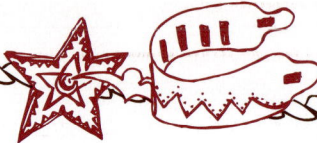

blush wine jelly

yields 4 to 6, half-pint jars

2	cups white Zinfandel wine	1	(3-ounce) package liquid fruit pectin (Do not use powdered pectin.)
3	cups sugar		

Combine wine and sugar in a large, non-aluminum saucepan over medium heat, stirring until sugar dissolves. Bring mixture to a simmer, but do not boil. Remove from heat and stir in pectin.

Pour into four to six hot, sterilized half-pint jars quickly, filling to ¼-inch from the top; wipe jar rims. Cover at once with metal lids, and screw on bands. Process jars in a water bath for 15 minutes to seal lids.

chocolate sauce

yields 3 cups

1	cup sugar	1¾	cups milk
¼	cup all-purpose flour	1	tablespoon butter or margarine
¼	cup cocoa powder	1	teaspoon vanilla extract
½	teaspoon salt		

Combine sugar, flour, cocoa, salt, milk and butter in a medium saucepan over medium heat. Cook, stirring constantly, until thickened. Remove from heat and stir in vanilla. Serve hot over ice cream. Cover and store remaining sauce in the refrigerator.

mopping sauce

yields 3 cups

1	cup ketchup	2	tablespoons sugar
1	cup strong black coffee	1	tablespoon cracked black pepper
½	cup Worcestershire sauce	½-1	tablespoon salt
¼	cup butter	1-2	jalapeños, chopped

Combine ketchup, coffee, Worcestershire, butter, sugar, pepper, salt and jalapeño in a saucepan over medium heat. Bring mixture to a boil; reduce heat and simmer for 30 minutes. Use to baste any type of grilled meats.

creamy cilantro sauce

yields 4 servings

1	(4-ounce) can green chiles	½	cup sour cream
½	cup heavy whipping cream	1	tablespoon chopped fresh cilantro

Place chiles in the container of a blender; process until smooth.

Combine chiles and cream in a small saucepan over medium-low heat. Bring to a boil; reduce heat and simmer.

Whisk in sour cream and cilantro. Cook until thoroughly heated.

Delicious served with beef or poultry.

mexican marinade

yields ⅔ cup

⅓ cup white wine vinegar	¼ teaspoon dried thyme
2 red or green chiles, seeded and chopped	¼ teaspoon ground cumin
	dash ground cloves
2 cloves garlic, minced	freshly ground black pepper

Combine all ingredients in a small bowl, stirring until well blended. Rub mixture into meat; cover with plastic wrap and refrigerate 6 hours or overnight. Cook as desired.

A hot and lightly spicy marinade that is suitable for pork, chicken or beef.

tart and spicy marinade

yields 1 cup

½ cup olive oil	1 jalapeño, chopped
3 tablespoons fresh lime juice	1 teaspoon garlic, minced
3 slices onion	

Combine oil, juice, onion, jalapeño and garlic in a large, plastic zip-top bag. Add meat; seal and refrigerate 24 hours prior to grilling.

asian marinade

yields enough for 4 servings

4	teaspoons crushed red pepper flakes	2	teaspoons peeled and grated fresh ginger
1	tablespoon olive oil	2	teaspoons chopped garlic
1	tablespoon sesame seed oil		

Combine pepper flakes, olive oil, sesame oil, ginger and garlic in a shallow container. Add meat; cover and marinade 30 minutes. If marinating longer, place in refrigerator until ready to cook.

Remove meat from marinade, discarding marinade. Cook as desired.

Easily doubled. This marinade is great on fresh tuna, red snapper fillets or shrimp. Also good on pork ribs and boneless chicken breasts.

red-hot fish batter

yields 4 cups

1	(12-ounce) bottle Trappy's Red Devil or other hot sauce	½	cup all-purpose flour
½-⅔	cup Cajun seasoning	2	tablespoons cayenne pepper
½	cup cornmeal		black pepper

Soak fish in hot sauce for 2 hours; drain.

Combine seasoning, cornmeal, flour, cayenne and pepper in a shallow bowl. Dredge fish in mixture and fry in hot oil.

Ingredient Substitutions

If a recipe calls for:	You may substitute:
1 cup all-purpose flour	1 cup plus 2 tablespoons cake flour OR 1 cup rolled oats OR 1 cup graham flour OR 1 cup rye flour OR 1½ cup bran OR 1½ cup bread crumbs OR ⅞ cup cornmeal

1 cup sifted self-rising flour	1 cup sifted all-purpose flour plus
	    1½ teaspoons baking powder and
	    ⅛ teaspoon salt

1 cup sifted cake flour	1 cup sifted all-purpose flour less 2 tablespoons
1 cup biscuit mix	1 cup flour plus 1½ teaspoons baking powder and 2 tablespoons shortening
2 tablespoons flour (for thickening)	1 tablespoon cornstarch OR ¾ ounce bread crumbs OR 7 egg yolks OR 3½ whole eggs

1 teaspoon baking powder	¼ baking soda plus ½ teaspoon cream of tartar
	OR ¼ teaspoon baking soda plus
	    ½ cup buttermilk or sour milk
	    (reduce liquid in recipe by ½ cup)
	OR 2 egg whites

1 tablespoon cornstarch	2 tablespoons all-purpose flour
1 package (2 teaspoons) active dry yeast	1 cake compressed yeast

If a recipe calls for:	You may substitute:
1 cup whole milk	¼ cup dry whole milk plus 1 cup water
	OR ¾ cup non-fat dry milk plus
	1 cup water and 3 tablespoons melted butter
	OR ½ cup evaporated milk plus ½ cup water
	OR 1 cup buttermilk plus ½ teaspoon baking soda
1 cup light cream	⅞ cup milk plus 3 tablespoons melted butter
1 cup heavy cream	¾ cup milk plus ⅓ cup melted butter
1 cup buttermilk or sour milk	1 cup milk plus 1 tablespoon lemon juice or
	vinegar; let stand 5 minutes
	OR 1 cup milk plus 1¾ teaspoons cream of tartar
1 cup heavy sour cream	1 cup plain yogurt
	OR ⅔ cup sour milk, buttermilk or plain yogurt
plus ⅓ cup melted butter	
	OR 1 cup evaporated whole milk and
	1 tablespoon lemon juice
1 cup thin sour cream	¾ cup sour milk, buttermilk or plain yogurt plus
	3 tablespoons melted butter
1 cup dark corn syrup	¾ cup light corn syrup plus ¼ cup light molasses
1 cup light or dark corn syrup	1¼ cups granulated or packed brown sugar
	plus ¼ cup additional liquid from recipe
1 cup powdered sugar	½ cup plus 1 tablespoon granulated sugar
1 cup light brown sugar	½ cup dark brown sugar plus ½ cup
	granulated sugar

If a recipe calls for:	You may substitute:
1 cup granulated sugar	1¾ cups powdered sugar OR 1 cup firmly packed brown sugar OR 1 cup superfine sugar
1 (1-ounce) square unsweetened chocolate	2 tablespoons cocoa plus ½ tablespoon butter OR ½ cup semisweet chocolate morsels, decreasing shortening by 1 tablespoon and decreasing sugar by ¼ cup OR 1 (1-ounce) envelope soft baking chocolate
3 (1-ounce) squares semisweet baking chocolate	½ cup semisweet chocolate morsels
¼ cup cocoa powder	½ cup (3 ounces) semisweet chocolate morsels decreasing shortening by 1 tablespoon and decreasing sugar by ¼ cup OR 1 (1-ounce) envelope soft baking chocolate

Food Storage

Food	Fresh or Dry	Canned	Refrigerated	Frozen
DAIRY:				
Butter			2 to 3 weeks	1 year
Cheese			2 to 8 months	1 year
Cheese (processed)			6 to 8 months	1 year
Milk			5 to 14 days	
Eggs			1 to 2 weeks	
MEAT:				
Bacon			1 to 2 weeks	3 months
Beef			2 to 7 days	1 year
Beef, ground			2 to 3 days	2 months
Lamb			2 to 7 days	1 year
Pork			3 to 7 days	3 months
Sausage			2 to 5 days	3 months
Chicken			2 to 5 days	3 months
Turkey			2 to 5 days	6 months
Fish			1 to 3 days	5 months
Ham			2 weeks	6 months
Cold cuts			3 to 7 days	3 months
NUTS AND BEANS:				
Dry beans	1 to 3 years		12-18 months	
Dry peas	1 to 3 years			
Peanut butter		6 months	12 to 18 months	
Nuts (unshelled)	1 year			
Nuts (shelled)	6 months	1 year	12 to 18 months	2 years
CEREAL, GRAINS AND BAKING PRODUCTS:				
Baked products	1 week			9 months
Baking mix	1 year			
Baking Powder	1 year			
Baking soda	1 year			
Bouillon	1 year			
Chocolate	2 years			
Cocoa powder	6 months	1 year	1 year	

Food	Fresh or Dry	Canned	Refrigerated	Frozen
Cornmeal (fresh)	2 months			
Cornmeal (degermed)	2 years			
Cornstarch	2 years			
Flour (white)	1 year			
Flour (whole grain)	4 months			1 year
Herbs (dried)	6 months			1 year
Rice	2 years			
Pasta (uncooked)	1 year			
Yeast	2 to 6 months			

FRUITS AND VEGETABLES:

Food	Fresh or Dry	Canned	Refrigerated	Frozen
Apples	1 month	1 year	1 to 6 months	1 year
Beans (green)	1 to 3 days	18 months	3 to 5 days	1 year
Berries	3 to 5 days	6 months	3 to 7 days	1 year
Cabbage			2 to 3 months	1 year
Carrots		18 months	1 to 3 weeks	1 year
Citrus fruits	3 to 5 days	6 months	3 to 5 days	1 year
Corn	1 day	18 months	2 to 3 days	1 year
Cranberries			1 week	1 year
Grapes			2 to 4 weeks	
Onions	1 to 6 months			
Peaches	3 to 5 days	18 months	7 to 10 days	1 year
Peas (green)	1 day	18 months	2 to 3 days	1 year
Pears	1 to 3 days	18 months	4 to 6 weeks	1 year
Pineapple	3 to 5 days	18 months	3 to 7 days	1 year
Potatoes	1 to 3 months	18 months	2 to 3 days	1 year
Spinach		18 months	2 to 5 days	1 year
Sweet potatoes	8 months	18 months		1 year
Tomatoes		18 months	4 to 6 days	

Herbs and Spices

Herbs are the fragrant leaves of annuals and perennials that do not have woody stems. Herbs include: basil, bay leaves, chervil, chives, dill, marjoram, mint, oregano, parsley, rosemary, sage, saffron, savory, tarragon, thyme.

Spices are the aromatic seasonings from the bark, buds, roots, seeds or stems of plants and trees. Spices include: allspice, anise, caraway, cayenne, cinnamon, cloves, cumin, dill, ginger, mace, mustard seeds, nutmeg, paprika, pepper, poppy seeds, saffron, sesame seeds, and turmeric

Herb bouquet: a blend of herbs wrapped in cheesecloth and tied at the top.

Classic bouquet: 2 sprigs fresh parsley, 1 sprig fresh thyme, bay leaf

Bouquet for beef: fresh basil, fresh parsley, bay leaf and clove

Bouquet for veal: fresh parsley, fresh thyme and lemon peel

Bouquet for lamb: fresh rosemary, fresh parsley and celery

Cajun Seasoning: garlic, onion, chiles, black pepper, mustard and celery

Fines herbs: a blend of parsley, chives, tarragon and chervil

Italian Seasoning: basil, oregano, marjoram, rosemary

Jamaica Jerk Seasoning: chiles, thyme, cinnamon, ginger, allspice, cloves, garlic, onion

Sweet herbs: thyme, sage, chives and mint

Tips and Hints

A tablespoon of fresh herbs is equivalent to 1 teaspoon dried.

Finely chopped or minced fresh herbs will release more flavor to food than whole leaves.

Fresh herbs lose flavor during cooking. Add fresh herbs during the last 15 minutes of cooking. Dried herbs are added early in preparation to allow flavors to develop.

Fresh herbs should be added early in cold preparations such as salad dressing and marinades to allow flavors to blend.

Store fresh herbs in the refrigerator. Wrap in damp paper towels and seal in an airtight bag for up to 5 days.

Crush or crumble dried herbs and spices to release more flavor during cooking.

To boost the flavor of dried herbs when using in a cold preparation, soak in just enough hot water to moisten before adding to recipe.

Purchase dried herbs and spices in small quantities. Herbs have a shelf life of only 4 to 6 months, but may be frozen up to a year.

Store dried herbs and spices in airtight containers away from heat, light and moisture. Check for freshness frequently as stale or rancid herbs and spices will ruin a dish.

Strong herbs such as rosemary, sage, basil or tarragon do not blend well as their flavors compete and overpower the dish.

When doubling or tripling a recipe, do not double or triple the amount of herbs and spices. Add 1½ times the amount, then season to taste.

If a recipe gives a range of measurement for herbs or spices, add the lower measurement first, then season to taste.

For maximum flavor, use freshly ground spices rather than ready ground.

Herb and Spice Chart

Herb	Description	Uses
basil	subtle, spicy, licorice-clove flavor	tomato dishes, sauces, salads, eggs, cheese, poultry, veal, pork, lamb, Italian dishes
bay leaf	aromatic leaf from a laurel tree, used whole and removed before serving	meat and seafood dishes, soups, vegetable dishes and sauces
chervil	dark green lacy leaves with anise flavor	seafood and egg dishes, soups, salads
chives	slender, green hollow stems with mild onion flavor	salads, soups, sauces, seafood and egg dishes
dill	feathery, green leaves with pungent flavor	pickles, salads, dressing, soups, chicken and seafood dishes
fennel	pale green feathery leaves	seafood and egg dishes, salads, Italian and Swedish dishes
marjoram	mild, oregano-like flavor	poultry, seafood, vegetable and egg dishes, salads, sauces, soups
mint	pungent, cool flavor	Lamb, fruit and vegetable dishes, desserts, jellies, sauces, salads
oregano	pungent and aromatic flavor	pasta, sauces, dressings, egg and and cheese dishes, Greek and Italian dishes
parsley	spicy, slightly bitter flavor	meat, seafood, poultry, salads, dressings, soups; used widely as a garnish
rosemary	slender needles with strong lemon-pine flavor	lamb, beef, poultry, egg dishes Italian and French dishes
sage	gray-green leaves with slightly musty flavor	pork, sausage, seafood, game, veal, poultry, stuffings, soups, sauces
savory	pungent aroma and flavor; found in summer and winter varieties	poultry, egg dishes, salads, stuffings
tarragon	aromatic, anise-like flavor	poultry, meat, seafood, salads, sauces, dressings, soups, marinades, French dishes

Spice	Description	Uses
thyme	pungent flavor	meat, poultry, seafood, soups, stuffings, dressings
allspice	flavor blend of clove, cinnamon and nutmeg	baked goods, fruit pies, pumpkin pie, pickles, soups, beef, lamb
anise	sweet licorice flavor	baked goods, fruit and vegetable salads, cheese, poultry, veal, shellfish, Mediterranean dishes
caraway seeds	delicate anise flavor	rye bread, sauerkraut, potato-cabbage dishes, beef, pork, cheese dishes
cardamom	black-brown seeds with warm, sweet flavor	baked goods, beverages, fruits, soups and curry dishes
cayenne pepper	spicy-hot ground red pepper	meat, chicken, pork ribs, sausages, eggs, chili, seafood, Mexican and Tex-Mex dishes
celery seeds	strong, pungent flavor	pickling, salads, egg and vegetable dishes, seafood dishes
chili powder	powdered mixture of hot, spicy peppers	meat, beans, rice, chili, Spanish, Mexican and Tex-Mex dishes
cinnamon	spicy bark found ground or in sticks	baked goods, desserts, beverages, pickles, fruits
cloves	dried, unopened flower bud with spicy, aromatic flavor; found whole or ground	baked goods, hot beverages; used whole to stud ham or oranges
coriander seeds	yellowish-tan seeds with perfumed, aromatic flavor	curries, soups, stews, pickling, Indian, Mexican, Caribbean and Asian dishes
curry powder	golden-yellow blend of several spices	chicken, lamb, seafood, cheese and egg dishes, Indian and Middle Eastern dishes
cumin	aromatic, nutty flavor	chicken, meat, chutney, Mexican and Tex-Mex dishes
fennel seeds	licorice flavor	sausage, seafood, salads, dressings, egg dishes and Swedish and Italian dishes

Spice	Description	Uses
garlic	multi-cloved bulb with strong, pungent aroma and flavor	widely used in meats, fish, poultry, salads, dressings, soups, sauces, Mediterranean dishes
ginger	irregularly shaped root with sharp, pungent flavor; can be found fresh, ground or crystallized	Asian dishes, baked goods, preserves, meat
mustard	sharp, spicy flavor	pickles, relishes, sauces and glazes, meat, poultry, fish dishes salad dressings and dips
nutmeg	mellow, spicy flavor	baked goods, beverages, soups vegetable and egg dishes
paprika	sweet, peppery flavor and dark red color	Hungarian and Spanish dishes; used widely as a garnish
black & white pepper	pungent, spicy flavor	used widely; use white pepper when a subtle flavor is desired or when black pepper specks should not be seen
poppy seeds	tiny blue-black seeds with nutty flavor	topping for baked goods, dressings, dips, pasta
saffron	pungent, slightly bitter flavor with reddish-yellow color; costly	seafood dishes, rice dishes, eggs, Spanish and French dishes
sesame seeds	slightly sweet, nutty flavor	topping for baked goods, salads, soups and casseroles
turmeric	yellow-orange color with pungent flavor	used in curry blends and pickling; substitutes for saffron

Wine Selection Guide

Type of Wine	Specific Wine	Serve With
Appetizer	Sherry, dry Vermouth, dry Port	appetizers, nuts, cheese
White Table Wines	Chablis, Sauterne, Pinot Grigio, Sauvignon Blanc, Chardonnay	seafood, poultry, lamb, veal, eggs, cheese, pork (except ham)
Red Table Wines	Blush	most foods, Asian foods, curry
	Claret, Merlot	beef, game, Italian food, Hawaiian food
	Chianti, Vino Rosso Cabernet Sauvignon Burgundy, Pinot Noir	red meat, cheese, roasts, game Italian food Cheese, Italian food, game, ham, roasts, steaks
Sparkling Wines	White Champagne	appetizers, seafood, poultry, desserts, cheese, celebrations
	Red Champagne	appetizers, roasts, game, desserts
Dessert Wines	Port, Muscatel, Riesling	desserts, fruits, nuts, cheese, cakes, pastries
	Gewürztraminer, Marsala Cream Sherry, Madeira	pastries

Wine

"Dry" wine means not sweet. "Sec" is the French term for a dry wine. "Demi-sec" is the term for semi-dry. The term "brut" indicates dry champagne or sparkling wine.

Store wine bottles on their sides to prevent the cork from drying out and shrinking. This lets air into the bottle that will spoil the wine.

Store wine in a dark, vibration-free space. The ideal temperature is 55°, but a range of 45° to 70° is acceptable if the temperature is consistent.

High temperatures causes wine to age and spoil prematurely.

White wine should be served between 50°and 55°. Cold temperature mute flavors; serve a lesser quality white wine colder.

White wine can be chilled in the refrigerator for 2 hours prior to serving. To speed-chill, place wine in a bucket of salted ice water for 20 minutes.

Red wines should be served at 65°, not at "room temperature". Today's homes have higher average room temperatures than years past.

To avoid wine drips, twist the bottle as you finish pouring while returning bottle to an upright position.

Wine glasses should be filled two-thirds full. There should be room to swirl the wine to release its bouquet. Pour 3- to 3½-ounce servings for dinner wines and champagne, and 2- to 2½-ounce servings for appetizer and dessert wines.

To prolong the flavor of an opened bottle of wine, decant into a smaller bottle or use one of the many wine-savor devices on the market. Air ruins the flavor of wine.

Some foods ruin the fine taste of wine: vinegary salad dressings, citrus fruits such as grape-fruits, oranges or lemons and oily fish.

Stain Removal

Try to remove a stain as soon as possible before laundering. Use cold water to flush away a stain before it has time to set. Cold water is usually best because hot water may permanently set a stain.

Gravy, sauces and meat juices: rinse item in cold water, then rub with mild soup. If stain remains, use an enzyme presoak solution or grease solvent.

Tomato stains: rinse with cold water and treat with an enzyme presoak before laundering

Butter, grease or oil: Place a dry cloth under the stain and rub area with hot, sudsy water. Blot with a grease solvent and launder.

Wine: pour cold water or club soda through the stain, rubbing gently until it disappears. Launder immediately. If you are unable to remove the item for immediate cleaning, rub salt on the stain and let stand until laundered.

Fruit juice: Blot with cold water. If stain has dried, pour boiling water through the stain and launder.

Jelly: rinse item in cold water and rub with a mild soap. Rinse and launder.

Tea and coffee: rinse with cold water or if possible, pour boiling water through stain. If coffee contained cream, blot with a grease solvent before laundering.

Dairy products: Rinse with cold water, then launder as usual. If stain persists, use a grease solvent before laundering.

Lipstick and cosmetics: rub stain with a mild liquid soap. If stain is still visible, use a laundry pre-treatment product or grease solvent and launder.

Candlewax: remove excess wax with a blunt knife. Place item between two clean towels and press with a warm iron. If stain persists, pour boiling water through the stain and blot with cleaning fluid before laundering.

Ink: If stain bleeds or runs when water is applies, continue to pour cold water through the stain until it disappears. If stain is not water soluble, use a laundry pre-treatment fluid or commercial ink remover.

Blood: rinse immediately with cold water. If stain persists, use an enzyme presoak for at least 30 minutes prior to laundering.

Mildew: launder item in hot water and dry in sunlight. If mildew is still present, pour buttermilk over stain, rinse and dry in the sun.

Rust: blot stain with a mixture of lemon juice and salt, rinse with cold water and dry in the sun. If stain persists, use a commercial rust remover.

Scorch marks: blot stain with a mixture of lemon juice and salt and let dry in the sun; launder as usual. If stain is still present try rubbing a freshly cut onion over scorch mark, rinse with cold water and launder as usual.

Contributors and Testers
Special Thanks

The Cookbook Committee wishes to thank the following contributors who have graciously shared their recipes or who have taken the time to enthusiastically join in this project. Many of the recipes where adapted or combined after extensive testing to make *Ropin' the Flavors of Texas* a cookbook for all to enjoy.

Nancy Aimone
Bertha Albert
Dorothy Alcorn
Diane Alexander
Bess Alkek
Laurie Alkek
Sallye Allen
Beth Antimarino
Gladys Averill
Melissa Bales
Carrie Bang
Elizabeth Barnes
Linda Ladig Bates
Vicki Bauknight
Virginia Berger
Martha Booth Bernhardt
Becky Berryhill
Gladys Bigelow
Carol Bauknight Bishop
JaNae Sterling Blackaller*
Johanna Bloom
Mary Katherine Borchers
Lorene Bothe
Richard Bothe
Barbara Briggs
Margy Briggs
Melanie Buchhorn
Karen Burnup
Allison Burrows
Brooke Callender
Jennifer Camet
Kathryn Cardinell
Kathleen W. Carey
Pam Chesak
Sandra Christian
Kim Cire
Cheryl Cliburn
Donna Cole
Muriel Cullen
Mary Ann Davis
Bernie Denison Seale

Aileen Devine
Babs Diebel
Trisha Easterling
Amy Eastham
Julie Bauknight Eaves
Kay Edwards
Sarah Eilers
Sharon Elder
Kathy Ellisor
Suzanne Foertsch
Sylvia Frank
Betty Frederick
Penni Gietz
Kacee Gonzales
Genevieve Goodpasture
Cheryl Green
Elizabeth Greeson
Laura Grunewald
Cheryl Guthrie
Dorothy Guthrie
Linda Massouh Hall
Jennifer Hartman
Jennifer Rode Hartman
Pama Hencerling
Donna Henderson
Sammie Sue Hendrix
Ginger Henke
Kelly Henke
Brenda Hermes
Betty Hill
Debbie Holzheauser
Janet Hutson
Gwen Jackson
Gladys Jackson-Averill
Jan Janota
Jerome Jenschke
Sue Jones
Gormeen Kamin
Sue Klapper
Ethel Klotzman
Rise Konarik

Betsy Coleman Kopecky
Jan Kyle
Judy Lamkin
Jill Lau
Robbie Lauger
Gaye Gilster Lee
Carol Weatherly Lilly
Mary Logan
Sarah Loud
Edwina Mabray
Elaine Malina
Jackie Marlow
J. Michael Mastej
Lucy Mastej
Martha Price Maxwell
Jane McCann
Kelly McCarty
Kay McCoy
Janeil McCrury
Sara McDowell
Wendy McHaney
Rebecca McKenzie
Sandra McKenzie
Michelle McNeill
Brooke Mercer
Camille Miller
Brigette Miori-Hogsed
Geanie W. Morrison
Mary Sue Koontz Nelson
Jamie Notz
Lorretta Owen
Lauran Pall
Joy Peavy
Karen Perez
Nancy Renaud
Janet Russell
Kathryn Kopecky Schaper
Vanessa Scheumack
Jill Schlein
Mary Schuenemann
Bernie Seale

Mary Ann Seale
Gwen Sheffield
Katherine Sinclair
Larry Smith
Myra Starkey
Dodie Arney Stofer
Lisa Alkek Stoika
Don Strange
Martha Tarkington
Mary Taylor
Shelly Tharp
Stephanie Thayer
Tenna Thompson
Shannon Tipton
Evelyn Tittizer
Cynthia Tucker
Tanna Villarreal
Kay Walker
Leslie Wall
Clyde Walrod
Mary K. Walrod
Karen Webb
Donna Welder
Heather Welder
Mary Wenske
Dolores White
Patti Wied
Sonya Williams
Kitty Wilson
Carol Wisdom
Natalie Alkek Wood
Doris Wuensche
Catherine Fossati Wyatt
Pam Younts
Liz Zowarka
Daphne Zuniga
Judy Zuniga
Fossati's Delicatessen
Taqueria Victoria
Plaza Club
Beijing Garden

Index

327

V

veal

W

Z

zucchini (also see squash)

Please send me _____ copies of *Ropin' the Flavors of Texas*   @ $22.95 each_____

Texas residents add sales tax   @ $ 1.89 each_____

Please add shipping and handling   @ $ 4.00 each_____

Total _____

Make checks payable to The Junior League of Victoria, Texas, Inc.

and send to:
The Junior League of Victoria, Texas, Inc.
202 North Main Street
Victoria, TX 77901

— —

Please send me _____ copies of *Ropin' the Flavors of Texas*   @ $22.95 each_____

Texas residents add sales tax   @ $ 1.89 each_____

Please add shipping and handling   @ $ 4.00 each_____

Total _____

Make checks payable to The Junior League of Victoria, Texas, Inc.

and send to:
The Junior League of Victoria, Texas, Inc.
202 North Main Street
Victoria, TX 77901

— —

Please send me _____ copies of *Ropin' the Flavors of Texas*   @ $22.95 each_____

Texas residents add sales tax   @ $ 1.89 each_____

Please add shipping and handling   @ $ 4.00 each_____

Total _____

Make checks payable to The Junior League of Victoria, Texas, Inc.

and send to:
The Junior League of Victoria, Texas, Inc.
202 North Main Street
Victoria, TX 77901

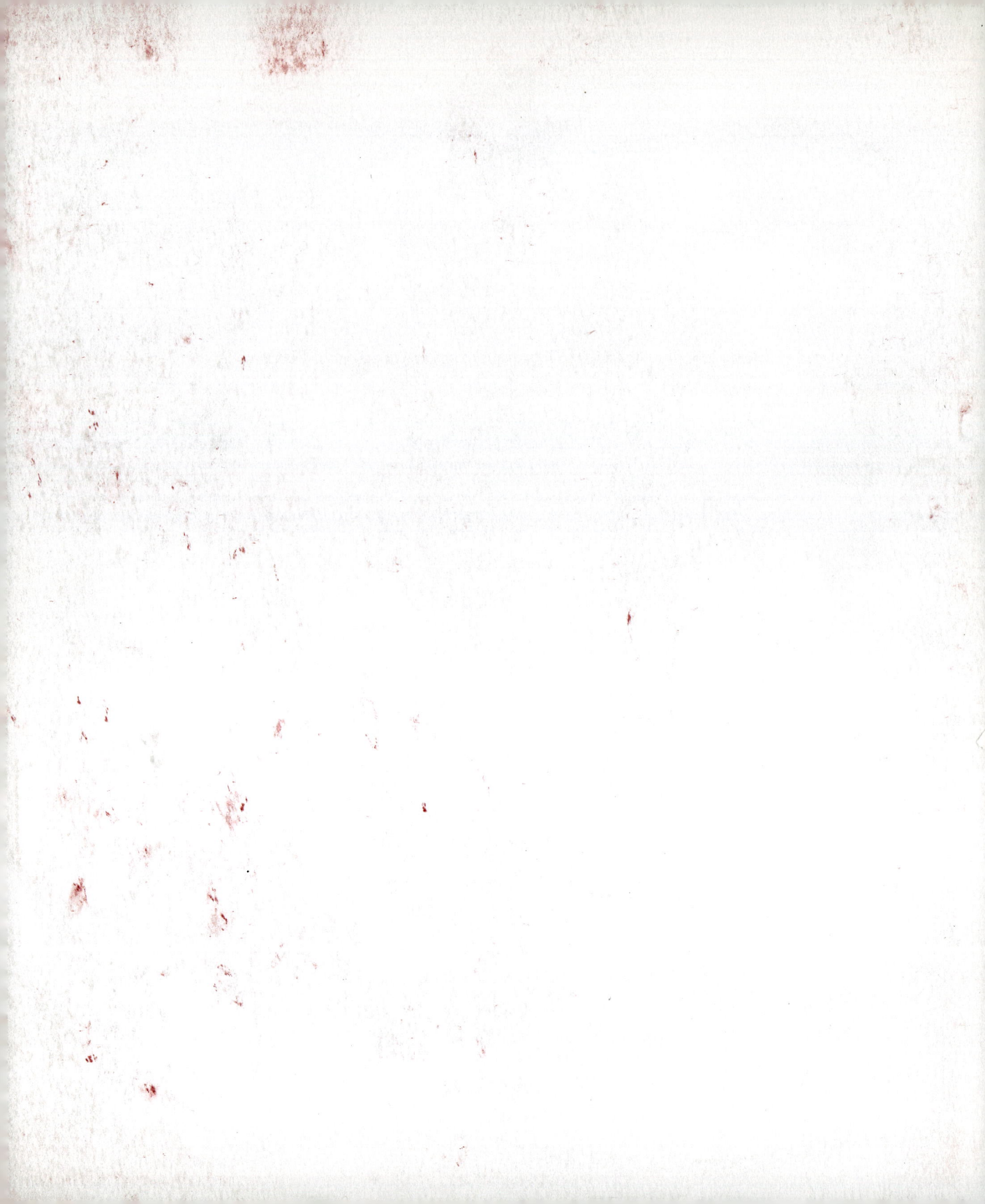